Talk About the Cover

Eagle

Eagle, eagle, spread your wings.

You can **SEE** so many things,

Soaring **HIGH** above the land.

An eagle's life is really **GRAND**.

How far can **YOU** soar?

ISBN 0-15-334262-5

6 7 8 9 10   048   10 09 08 07 06

Authors
Alma Flor Ada • F. Isabel Campoy • Yolanda N. Padrón • Nancy Roser

⋐Harcourt

Orlando   Austin   Chicago   New York   Toronto   London   San Diego

Visit *The Learning Site!*
www.harcourtschool.com

UNIT
1
SELF-DISCOVERY

Self-Discovery

Review Vocabulary with a Play
STORIES ON STAGE

Unit
Review

CONTENTS

UNIT 2 WORKING TOGETHER

Working Together

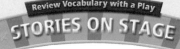

Review Vocabulary with a Play

STORIES ON STAGE

3

CONTENTS

UNIT 3
GROWTH AND CHANGE

Growth and Change

Review Vocabulary with a Play
STORIES ON STAGE

CONTENTS

UNIT 4 CREATIVITY

Creativity

Review Vocabulary with a Play

★ STORIES ON STAGE ★

Communities

CONTENTS

Explorations

Use What You Know

> **W**olves are part of the dog family, but they live in the wild. Wolves are very smart animals. They live in packs and hunt together. Wolves can smell things and hear things from far away.

■ **Think about expressions**

"I think *live in packs* means that wolves live together."

■ **Use prior knowledge**

"I know what dogs look like. Wolves must look like dogs."

■ **Reason**

"If wolves can hear things and smell things from far away, they are probably good hunters."

Find Help

Whales are mammals that live in the ocean. They look like giant fish. There are many kinds of whales. Some whales can weigh as much as twenty elephants.

■ **Use a computer**

"A computer can help me learn more about whales."

■ **Use books**

"The encyclopedia says that mammals are warm-blooded animals."

■ **Ask for help**

"I can ask a teacher, friend, or family member how to say the word *mammals.*"

Make Connections

> **K**atie can't wait to visit her grandparents in Maine. She lives in Florida, where it is warm most of the year. It is autumn now, so Katie's grandparents remind her to bring a sweater.

■ **Reuse language**

"I say *I can't wait* when I'm excited about something. I think Katie is excited to visit her grandparents."

■ **Use synonyms**

Another word for *lives* is *resides.* Another way to say *autumn* is *fall.*

■ **Compare and contrast**

Maine and Florida both have beaches. Maine is colder than Florida, and fewer people live there.

Picture It

> **W**hen my brother was a baby, he did not have hair. He couldn't speak, either. I was much bigger than he was! Now my brother has thick brown hair. He never stops talking, and he is very tall!

■ **Make pictures in your head**

as a baby . . .

now . . .

■ **Describe it**

"Telling someone else about a subject can help me picture it and remember it."

■ **Use actions**

"I can raise my arm to show how tall someone is."

11

Look for Patterns

■ Use rhyme

"*Knack* and *whack* both have *ack*. I am sure they rhyme. Knowing *knack* will help me read *whack*."

■ Use repetition

"*Give the dog a bone* repeats in this rhyme. I think *This old man came rolling home* also repeats."

■ Think about word families

"I know the letters *kn* in the word *knee* stand for the *n* sound. I can use this to read the words *knick* and *knack*."

> This old man, he played one,
> He played knick-knack on my thumb,
> With a knick-knack, paddy whack,
> Give the dog a bone,
> This old man came rolling home.
>
> This old man, he played two,
> He played knick-knack on my shoe,
> With a knick-knack, paddy whack,
> Give the dog a bone,
> _____.

Set a Purpose

Exercise is good for you. Team sports can make exercising fun for everyone. Some people enjoy playing basketball, football, or soccer. No matter what sport you like best, all sports are a good way to exercise.

- **Purpose for reading**

  "I want to find out about ways to exercise."

- **Purpose for speaking**

  "I want to get people to sign up for a team sport."

- **Purpose for writing**

  "I want to write a report about team sports."

- **Purpose for listening**

  "I will listen to find out more about exercise."

mirror

dresser

footstool

14

What Do I See?

I'm looking in the mirror
And who do I see?
Someone is looking
Back at me.
Who is in the mirror?
Who could it be?
What do you know—
That someone is ME!

*Sing to the tune of
"I'm a Little Teapot."*

chest

15

Word Clues

When you read a word you don't know, you can look for **word clues** to help you understand its meaning. Other words and sentences nearby can often help you figure out the word.

The boy received a <u>medal</u> for winning the race. It was shiny, and it hung on a blue ribbon around his neck.

The words in the second sentence tell you more about what a *medal* is.

Word	Context Clues	Meaning
medal	shiny hung on a blue ribbon	prize for winning

► Read the paragraph below. Look for clues in the paragraph to help you figure out the meaning of the underlined word.

Emma wanted to go to the family reunion, but she was worried. All of her <u>relatives</u> would be there. She had four grandparents, two aunts, three uncles, and ten cousins. That was a lot of people!

On a separate sheet of paper, copy the chart below. Write the clues that tell you the meaning of the word *relatives*.

Word	Context Clues	Meaning

Vocabulary POWER

Today Is Our Birthday! ▼

VOCABULARY

celebrate

city

break

gifts

coast

feast

candles

A birthday is a time to **celebrate** with friends. Sometimes people get special **gifts** on their birthdays.

The ten **candles** on this cake mean that someone is ten years old.

18

We had a **feast** with many different kinds of food.

A **city** is a place where many people live and work. This city is on the **coast**. It is near the sea.

If you press too hard as you write, you might **break** your pencil.

Today Is Our Birthday!

Everyone has a birthday. These children live in different parts of the world. They celebrate their birthdays in different ways. For all of them, birthdays are fun!

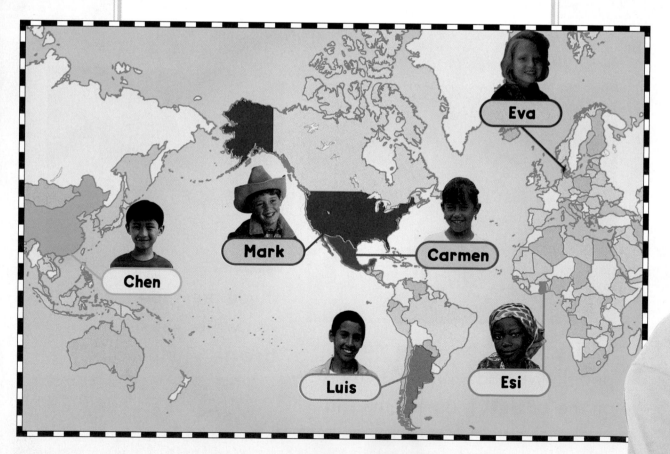

This is Carmen. She lives in Mexico City, a large city in central Mexico. Carmen and her friends celebrate Carmen's birthday with a piñata. They try to break the piñata so that the candy and gifts will fall out. This birthday celebration is fun for everyone!

Mexico

This is Chen. He lives in Hong Kong, a large city on the south coast of China. Every year, at Chen's birthday dinner, his mother serves a bowl of long noodles. Everyone wishes Chen a life that is long, just like the noodles!

China

This is Luis. He lives in Buenos Aires, a large city in Argentina. Luis is nine years old today. At his birthday party, his brother will gently pull on his ear nine times. Children get one pull for each year.

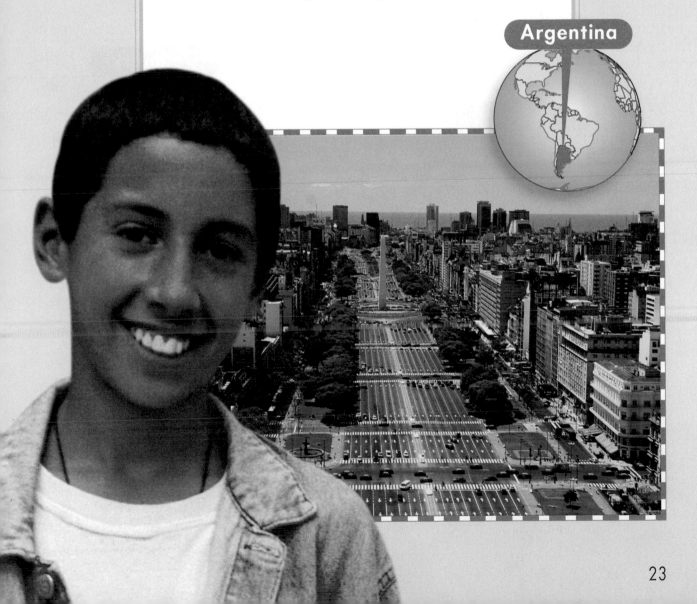

Argentina

This is Eva. Her home is in Denmark, a country in northern Europe. Everyone in the village knows it is Eva's birthday because a birthday flag hangs outside her window! When Eva woke up this morning, there were presents around her bed. Eva is happy that everyone remembered her special day.

Denmark

This is Esi. She lives in Ghana, a country on the west coast of Africa. Each year, people celebrate their birthdays with others who were born on the same day of the week. Esi was born on a Sunday, so she celebrates at a feast honoring people born on Sunday.

Ghana

This is Mark. He lives in Tucson, Arizona. Arizona is a state in the southwestern United States. Mark celebrates his ninth birthday with his friends and family. They sing "Happy Birthday" to him while he blows out the nine candles on his birthday cake.

United States

Families who come to the United States from other countries share their birthday celebrations with others. Some families like to make up new ways to celebrate. People around the world celebrate birthdays in many ways. How do you celebrate yours?

Related Vocabulary

This Is How We Celebrate

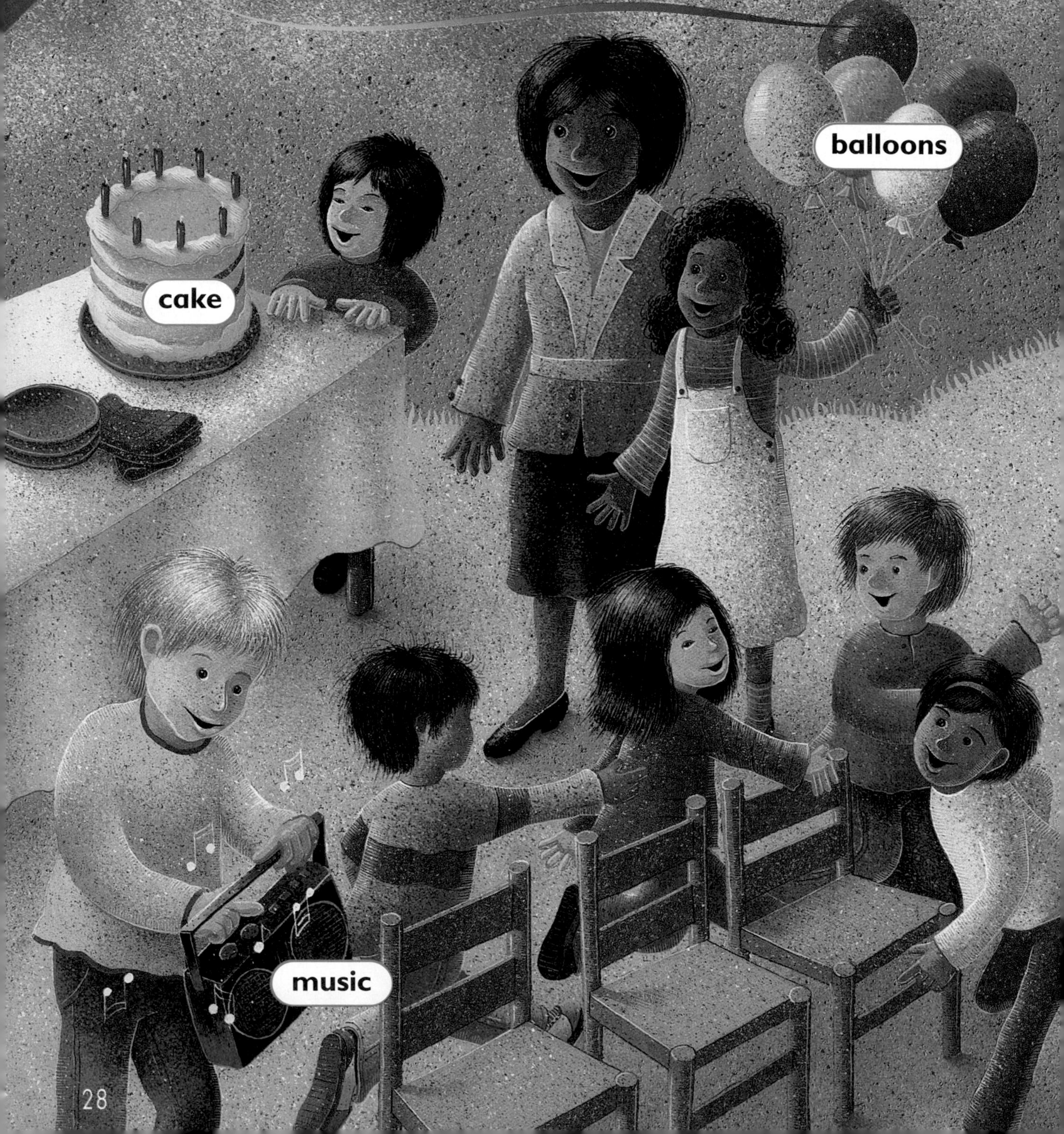
balloons
cake
music

piñata

presents

Think Critically

1. What are three ways people around the world celebrate birthdays?

2. How are birthday celebrations in Mexico and the United States the same?

3. How do you know the children in this selection enjoy their birthdays?

4. How would you choose to celebrate your birthday? Why?

Vocabulary POWER

Families, Families ▼

VOCABULARY

sisters

brothers

people

babies

new

laughing

singing

Lisa and Lori are **sisters**. They have the same mother and father. **People** from the same family sometimes look like each other.

These **brothers** enjoy reading together.

These **babies** play with toys. They all wear **new** shoes.

The family in this picture is **laughing** and having fun.

These people are **singing** a song.

Families, Families

by Dorothy and Michael Strickland

FAMILIES, FAMILIES
All kinds of families.
Mothers and fathers,
Sisters and brothers,
Aunts and uncles,
     And cousins, too.

33

FAMILIES, FAMILIES
All kinds of families.
People who live with us,
People who care for us,
Grandmas and grandpas,
And babies, brand new.

FAMILIES, FAMILIES
All kinds of families.
Coming and going,
Laughing and singing,
Caring and sharing,
And loving you.

Family Tree

grandmother grandfather

aunt uncle

father

cousin cousin

me

grandmother grandfather

mother aunt uncle

brother sister cousin

Think Critically

1 Who are some of the family members in this poem?

2 How do you think the author feels about families?

3 How are some families different? How are some families the same?

4 Choose one picture from the poem and tell why you like it.

Vocabulary POWER

More Friends, More Fun ▼

VOCABULARY

catch

friend

fun

throw

run

ropes

jump

long

Michael is going to **throw** a baseball.

This baseball player is trying to **catch** a ball. He has to reach a **long** way.

Maria loves to **jump**. Sometimes she skips two **ropes** at one time.

Carmen can **run** fast when she plays soccer.

Brian and his **friend** are playing a game. They are having **fun**.

More Friends, More Fun

You can't play catch
With only one.
I need a friend
To have some fun.

"This is no fun."

Come on and throw
The ball to me.
We'll run the bases—
One, two, three!

We have the ropes,
But we need friends
To jump them while
We turn the ends.

In fact, we'd like
It very much
If you'd jump in
For double Dutch!

It's hard to ride
A bike this long.
I need some friends
To ride along.

With lots of feet
To pedal fast,
The bike will start
To move at last!

I need some help
To reach the ground!
I wish I had
Some friends around.

"How do I land
this thing?"

Hurray, I'm saved!
My problem ends
With thanks to all
My helpful friends.

Think Critically

1. What does the poem tell you about having friends? Why are they important?

2. How does the elephant feel when the mice come to help? How do you know?

3. What happens when the alligator's friends join him?

4. How do your friends help you?

Vocabulary POWER

Max ▼

VOCABULARY

baseball

team

school

watch

teacher

stretches

clock

late

Will Chris hit the **baseball**?

I like to **watch** my sister play soccer.
Her **team** won first place.

The students in this **school** learn how to dance. This **teacher** shows her students each step.

A **clock** shows you what time it is. Watch the clock so you will not be **late** for the game!

Roberto **stretches** every day after he runs.

MAX

story and pictures by Rachel Isadora

Max is a great baseball player. He can run fast, jump high, and hardly ever misses a ball. Every Saturday he plays with his team in the park.

On Saturday mornings he walks with his sister
Lisa to her dancing school. The school is on the
way to the park.

One Saturday when they reach the school, Max
still has lots of time before the game is to start. Lisa
asks him if he wants to come inside for a while.

Max doesn't really want to, but he says O.K.
Soon the class begins. He gets a chair and sits
near the door to watch.

The teacher invites Max to join the class, but
he must take off his sneakers first.

He stretches at the *barre*.

He tries to do the split.

And the *pas de chat*. He is having fun.

Just as the class lines up to do leaps across the
floor, Lisa points to the clock. It is time for Max
to leave.

Max doesn't want to miss the leaps. He waits
and takes his turn.

Then he must go.

He leaps all the way to the park.

He is late. Everybody is waiting for him.

He goes up to bat.
Strike one!

He tries again.
Strike two!

And then . . . A home run!

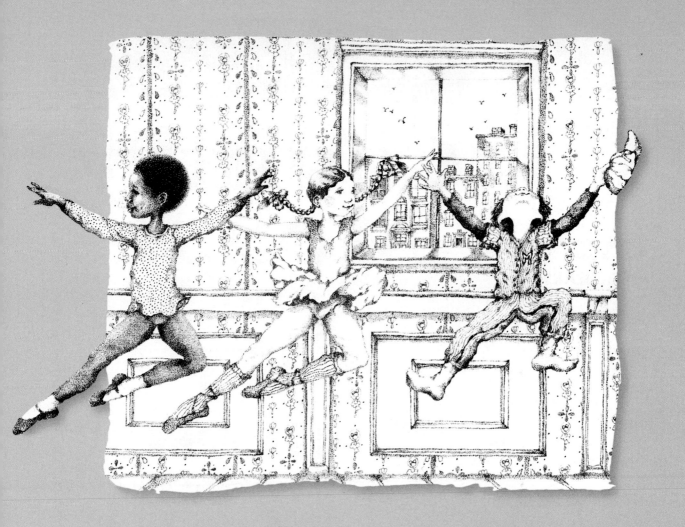

Now Max has a new way to warm up for the game on Saturdays. He goes to dancing class.

Think Critically

1 Does Max like his sister's dancing class? How do you know?

2 How does dance class help Max at the end of the story?

3 Why is Max late for his baseball game?

4 Tell about a time you tried something new.

Review Vocabulary with a Play

STORIES ON STAGE

Country Mouse and City Mouse

Characters

Narrator

Paco

Rico

Bird

Cat

Scene 1

Setting: The country

Narrator: Rico lives in the city. Today he is going to the country to visit Paco. Paco is Rico's best friend.

Rico: Thanks for inviting me to the country, Paco.

Paco: It's good to see you again, Rico! Let's pick wild berries for dinner. Then we'll have a delicious feast!

Rico: That sounds like fun!

Narrator: Rico and Paco walk to some berry bushes. Rico nibbles on a berry.

Rico: The fruit in the country is delicious! In the city, I get fruit from the grocery store.

Narrator: Suddenly, a giant bird swoops down and takes the berry from Rico. Then it flies back to its tree.

Bird: Leave my bushes alone! Find your own berries!

Narrator: The frightened mice run back to Paco's home as fast as they can.

Rico: It's much easier to get food in the city! We'll go there tomorrow, and I will show you.

Scene 2
Setting: The city, the next day

Narrator: The two friends travel to visit Rico's home in the city.

Paco: Look at those tall buildings! There are so many people here. The city is not quiet like the country.

Rico: Let's go to my home and get something to eat. It's getting late now. We've had a long trip, and I'm hungry! I'll show you how easy it is to get food in the city!

Narrator: Rico takes Paco to his home in the kitchen wall of an apartment. Rico tells Paco that the food is in a cupboard above the counter.

Paco: How will we get up there?

Rico: Just watch what I do and follow me.

Narrator: Rico and Paco begin climbing up to the cupboard. They don't notice the cat watching them.

Cat: Get away from that cupboard, you two! Find your own food!

Narrator: The mice run quickly to Rico's home in the wall.

Paco: That was close! Getting food in the city isn't always so easy, is it?

Rico: You're right—it's not. Tomorrow morning I'll take you to a place you might like.

Scene 3

Setting: The city park, the next day

Narrator: Rico wants Paco to feel at home in the city, so he takes him to a big park.

Paco: Look at all the trees! The park is quiet, like my home in the country.

Rico: It's like having the country in the city!

Narrator: Rico and Paco watch people throw bread to the birds. Children are laughing and playing together.

Paco: I see now that the city can be fun, but I'll always be a country mouse.

Rico: I had fun in the country, too! The berries there were delicious, but I will always be a city mouse.

Rico and Paco: Best of all, we'll always be friends!

Review Activities

Think and Respond

1 What did you learn about yourself from the people you read about in this unit?

2 What special events does your family celebrate? How are they like the celebrations in this unit?

3 How are families the same? How can they be different?

4 Why are some games more fun when more people play?

5 What kind of person is Max? Explain.

LANGUAGE STRUCTURE REVIEW

Make Introductions

With a group, talk about the different things that people say when they meet a new person. Stand in a circle with a group of classmates. Introduce yourself to the person standing to your left. That person will reply to you and then turn to the next person and introduce himself or herself. Take turns until everyone in the circle has been introduced.

VOCABULARY REVIEW

Do a Sentence Swap

Form two groups. Each group chooses four Vocabulary words. Make sure no one in the other group knows what your words are!

Work with your group to use each Vocabulary word in a sentence. Write the sentences on strips of paper. Next, cut apart all the words in each of the sentences. Put the words for each sentence into an envelope. Trade envelopes with the other group.

Each group should work to put the sentences together. Play again until each group has used all the Vocabulary words.

This scientist is putting a **sample** of something into a bottle so she can study it. She wears **gloves** to protect her hands.

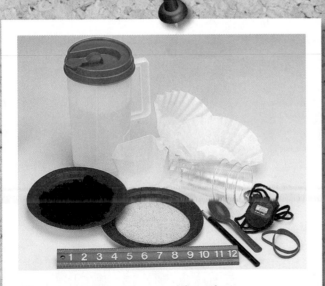

Our teacher brought this **equipment** for our science project. He cleaned water by pouring it through a **filter**.

A **clipboard** holds paper. When your paper is clipped to the board, you can write standing up.

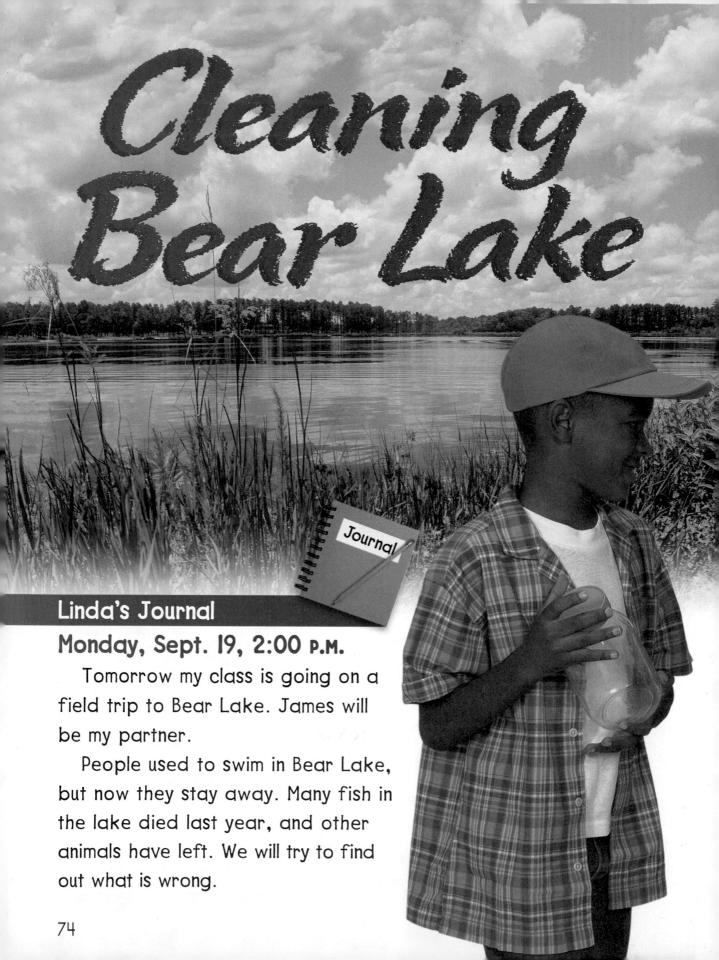

Cleaning Bear Lake

Linda's Journal

Monday, Sept. 19, 2:00 P.M.

Tomorrow my class is going on a field trip to Bear Lake. James will be my partner.

People used to swim in Bear Lake, but now they stay away. Many fish in the lake died last year, and other animals have left. We will try to find out what is wrong.

Tuesday, Sept. 20, 9:30 A.M.

On the bus we talked about our plans again. Our team will test a sample of the water from the lake. Other teams will look for wildlife. Some students will record the kinds of trash they find.

We have all our equipment in our backpacks. We're each taking a clipboard with paper and a pencil. We also have a jar with a lid, safety glasses, and gloves.

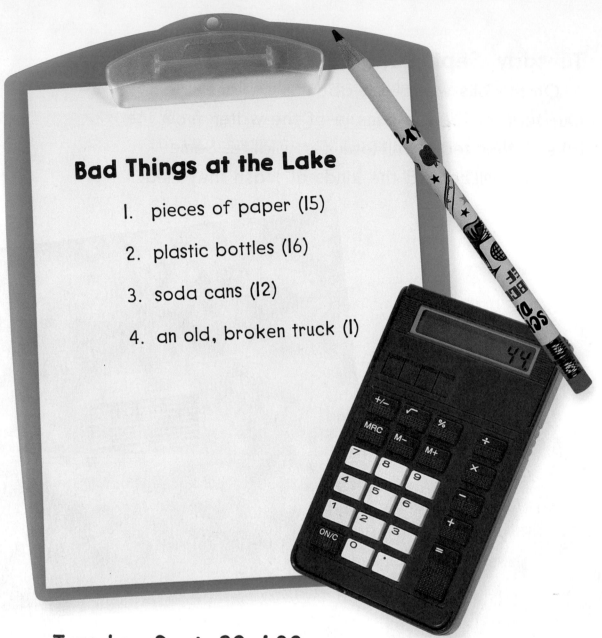

Bad Things at the Lake

1. pieces of paper (15)
2. plastic bottles (16)
3. soda cans (12)
4. an old, broken truck (1)

Tuesday, Sept. 20, 1:30 P.M.

At the lake we saw a few dead fish. An old, broken truck was in the water. The lake smelled very bad!

Our teacher, Mrs. Lawson, helped James and me fill our jar with water. The wildlife teams counted the ducks and other wild animals we saw. Another team listed the bad things we saw in the water.

Wednesday, Sept. 21, 10:30 A.M.

This morning, James and I put on gloves before doing our test. Mrs. Lawson helped us pour our water sample through a filter into another jar. The filter got very dirty! It showed pieces of plastic mixed with dirty oil. Mrs. Lawson said the oil may have come from the broken truck.

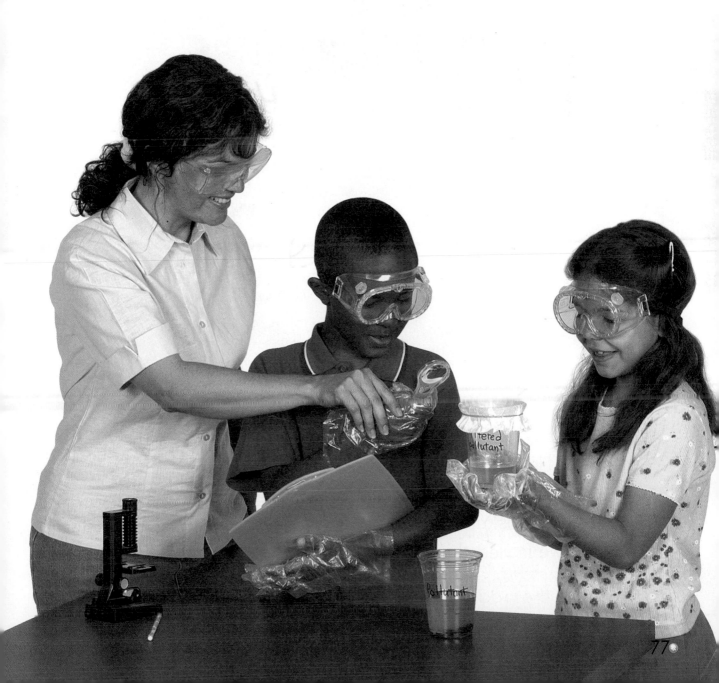

Mrs. Lawson's Class
Valley Elementary School
Middle Town, WA ,98109

Mayor Sharon Thomas
City Hall
Middle Town, WA 98109

Tuesday, Sept. 27, 10 A.M.

We finished our class report about Bear Lake. We decided to send it to the mayor. We wrote a letter and asked her to help us clean up the lake. Then we mailed the report and the letter. Now we will wait to see how Bear Lake can be cleaned.

Tuesday, May 12, 9:00 A.M.

Bear Lake is being cleaned up! The mayor was happy to help us. She had a Clean-Up Day and lots of people worked together to pick up the trash. She had signs put up telling people to keep the lake clean. The old truck was taken away. The mayor wrote us a letter, too. She thanked us for caring.

Now the fish and the birds will come back. We hope that people will soon be able to swim in the water. Bear Lake will be beautiful again!

At the Lake

dragonfly

life vest

fishing pole

net

bucket

sunfish

ducks

paddles

canoe

Think Critically

1 How do the students help clean up Bear Lake?

2 How might the students prove that the lake is cleaner?

3 How do you know the community cares about Bear Lake?

4 Is there a place near you that needs to be cleaned up? What could you do to make this happen?

Ant Cities ▼

VOCABULARY

hill

work

nest

tunnels

busy

seeds

eggs

adults

People do many kinds of **work**. These women are **busy** choosing colors and materials for a house.

The **eggs** in this **nest** belong to a robin.

Pumpkin **seeds** are very good to eat. What other kinds of seeds can you eat?

Children learn about ponies from these **adults**.

Goats like to eat grass on the top of this **hill**.

Some trains run in underground **tunnels**.

ANT CITIES

written and illustrated by Arthur Dorros

When it is sunny, the top of the nest gets warm.

When it rains, water runs off the hill.

If it gets too wet near the top of the nest, the ants move below.

In winter the ants hibernate in a deep room away from the cold. They stay together in a ball to keep warm.

▼

Have you seen ants busy running over a hill of dirt? They may look like they are just running around. But the ants built that hill to live in, and each ant has work to do.

Some ants may disappear into a small hole in the hill. The hole is the door to their nest.

These are harvester ants. Their nest is made of lots of rooms and tunnels. These little insects made them all.

Underneath the hill there may be miles of tunnels and hundreds of rooms. The floors are worn smooth by thousands of ant feet. It is dark inside the nest. But the ants stay cozy.

In the rooms of the nest, worker ants do many different kinds of work. It is like a city, a busy city of ants.

Some ants have brought in food to the ant city. These harvester ants like seeds.

A worker ant cracks the husks off the seeds. Another worker will take the husks outside to throw away.

The ants chew the seeds to get the juices out. Then they feed the juices to the other ants.

Other workers store seeds for the ants to eat another time.

Not all ants store food. But harvester ants do.

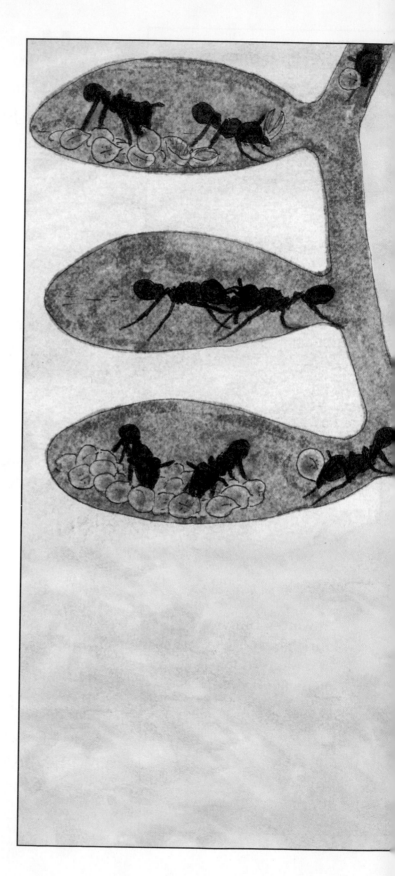

In one room of the nest, a queen ant lays eggs. Workers carry the eggs away to other rooms to take care of them.

Each ant city has to have at least one queen. Without a queen there would be no ant city. All the other ants in the ant city grow from the eggs the queen lays.

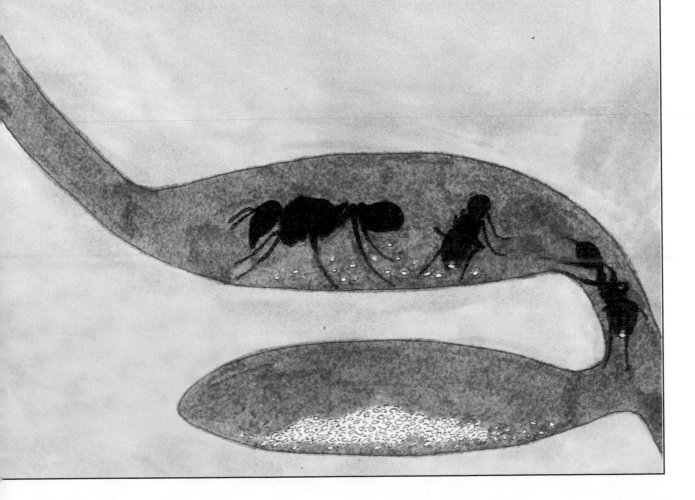

At first the tiny eggs grow into larvae. The worker ants feed the larvae and lick them clean so they will grow well.

The larvae grow into pupae. The workers keep grooming the pupae until they grow into adults.

The queen ant lays thousands and thousands of eggs. Most of the eggs grow into worker ants. There may be only one queen ant in an ant city, but there can be many thousands of workers.

Queen

The queen is usually bigger than the other ants. She lays eggs that grow into:

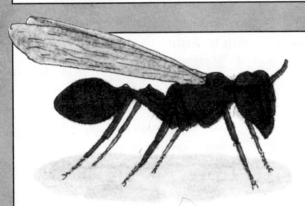

New Queens

New queens have wings. They use them to fly away to try to start new ant cities. Their wings drop off, and then the queens lay eggs.

Workers

Workers are all females. They do the work in the ant city. They will also fight to protect the nest.

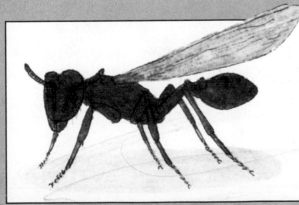

Males

Males don't live in the nest for long. They fly away with the new queens.

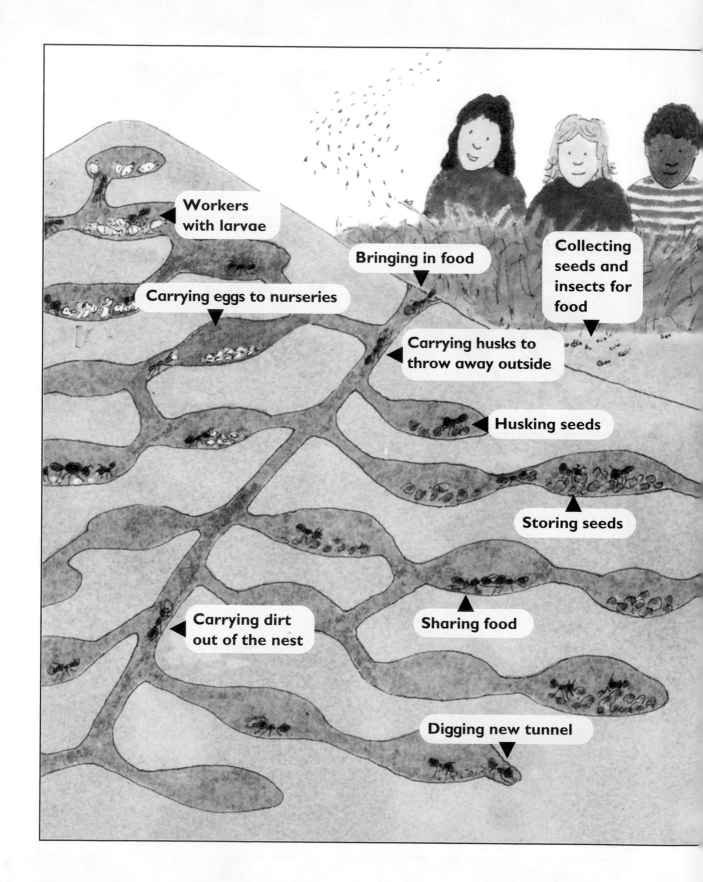

The queen doesn't tell the workers what to do. But the workers are busy. Each ant has work to do. Ants work together to keep the whole ant city alive.

Workers make the nest bigger by digging new rooms and tunnels. They use their feet to dig like tiny dogs. Workers pick up pieces of dirt in their jaws and "beards" and carry them outside.

Dirt from the digging is what makes the anthill. Ants are great diggers and builders. Imagine all the tiny pieces of dirt it takes to build a hill two feet high.

Out around the harvester anthill, workers look for food. Harvester ants mostly eat seeds. But sometimes they eat insects, too.

Ants can bite and sting other insects to capture them or to protect themselves. Be careful, because some kinds of ants can bite or sting you, too. Harvester ants will bite or sting if you disturb their nest.

Ants use their antennas to help them find food. They touch and smell with their antennas.

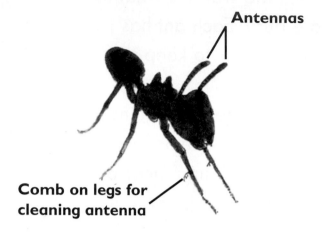

Antennas

Comb on legs for cleaning antenna

If one ant finds food, others follow. Soon there will be a lot of ants carrying away lunch.

If one ant can't carry something, others may help. But each worker ant is strong. An ant can lift as much as fifty times its own weight. If people could lift like that, we could each lift a car.

The workers carry the food back to the ant city. Ants share the food they find.

Ants eat many foods. But different kinds of ants like different foods. There are over 10,000 kinds of ants.

Formica ants mostly eat juices that they suck from insects they kill.

Cornfield ants like to eat the sweet juices, or "honeydew," they get from aphids. Aphids suck the juices from plants. Then the ants "milk" the aphids for honeydew.

Carpenter ants especially like sweet juices they can get from insects, and from plants, too.

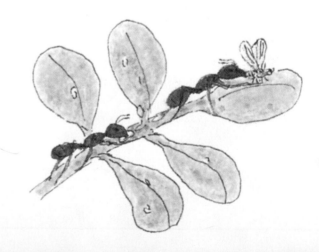

Thief ants eat sweets and other food they find in people's houses and lying about.

Leaf-cutting ants (parasol ants) make underground gardens with leaves they cut. They grow mushrooms in the gardens for food.

Army ants travel in large groups like armies. They devour huge numbers of insects, including termites.

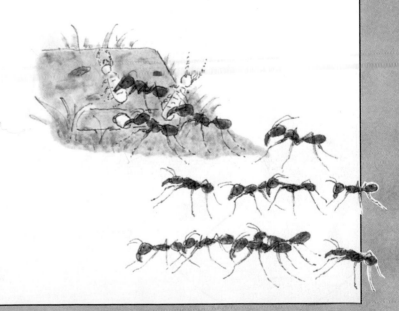

The different kinds of ants have found many ways to make their cities, so they can live in many kinds of places.

Janitor ants make their nests in hollowed-out tree twigs. The soldier janitor ant—a kind of worker ant—has a big, plug-shaped head it can use for a door.

Many kinds of ants make hills or mounds. If you haven't seen harvester anthills, maybe you've seen the round-topped hills that formica ants make. Sometimes they cover their hills with thatch.

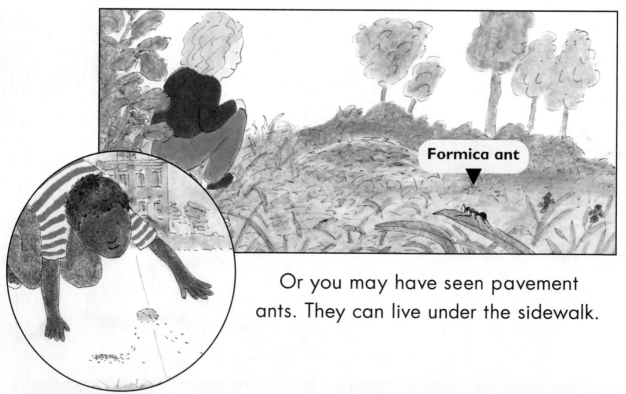

Formica ant

Or you may have seen pavement ants. They can live under the sidewalk.

Or carpenter ants, who build their nests in rotting wood.

There are small ant cities with just a few ants. There are big ant cities with many, many ants. Ants have been found at the tops of the highest buildings and on ships at sea.

Ants can make their cities almost anywhere. Look around and you'll probably find an ant city, busy with ants.

Think Critically

❶ How do ants help each other in ant cities?

❷ How are worker ants and queen ants different?

❸ How do you know that ants are hard workers?

❹ Which fact about ants surprised you the most?

Vocabulary POWER

The Great Big Enormous Rock ▼

VOCABULARY

animals

island

large

mountain

rock

picnic

push

together

There are many **animals** on the farm, but Mandy likes this cat best.

An **island** has water on all sides.

This mountain climber sits on a **rock** to rest. **Large** rocks like these are called boulders.

The top of this **mountain** is covered with snow.

My aunt likes to **push** my grandmother in her wheelchair.

The people in this family enjoy spending time **together**. They are having a **picnic**.

The Great Big Enormous ROCK

retold by Celia Barker Lottridge

Once there were four animals who lived on an island.

One was a very slow animal. A turtle!

One was a long, thin, slithering animal. A snake!

One was a small animal who hopped everywhere. A rabbit!

And one was a very large animal with flapping ears. An elephant!

Right in the middle of the island there was a tall mountain. On top of the tall mountain was a great big enormous rock. It was so big that it covered the top of the mountain.

The four animals looked at the rock every day. They said, "If that rock wasn't there we could climb the mountain and have a picnic." But every day the enormous rock was still there.

One day the turtle said, "I will climb the mountain and push the rock off the top." So up the mountain he went, *creepy, creepy, creepy*. When he got to the top he put the edge of his shell under the rock and he pushed and he pushed and he pushed. But the great big enormous rock did not budge.

Then the snake said, "I'll try, too." So up the mountain she went, *slither, slither, slither*. She coiled herself up like a spring and she pushed her tail against the rock. She pushed and she pushed and she pushed. But the great big enormous rock did not budge.

The rabbit said, "Now it's my turn." Up the mountain he went, *boing, boing, boing*. He put his strong back feet against the rock and he pushed and he pushed and he pushed. But the great big enormous rock did not budge.

The elephant laughed. "I'm the one to move the rock," she said. Up the mountain she went, *tromp, tromp, tromp*. She put her shoulder against the rock and she pushed and she pushed and she pushed. But the great big enormous rock did not budge.

The four animals looked at each other. "We will try it all together," they said. So the turtle pushed with his shell, the snake pushed with her tail, the rabbit pushed with his back feet, and the elephant pushed with her shoulder.

They pushed and they pushed and they pushed. They pushed again. And the great big enormous rock went *bumpity, bumpity, bumpity, bumpity,* CRASH! and it broke into a million pieces at the bottom of the mountain.

And the four animals sat down on top of their mountain and had a picnic.

Think Critically

1. Why do the animals wish that the rock was not on top of the mountain?

2. What is different about the way each animal goes up the mountain?

3. How can you tell that this story is a fable?

4. Would you do this much work to have a picnic? Why or why not?

Vocabulary POWER

The Family Business ▼

VOCABULARY

store

groceries

vegetables

flowers

neighborhood

lemonade

basket

garden

Brittany and Becky like to help their mother buy **groceries**. In this **store** there are many kinds of milk.

We buy fresh fruits and **vegetables** at the market each week.

My mother grows **flowers** in our backyard. She cuts them and puts them in a **basket**.

There are few trees in this **neighborhood**.

The plants in our **garden** need plenty of water.

Lemonade is a drink made from lemon juice, water, and sugar.

THE FAMILY BUSINESS

Today is Mother's Day. My big brother Rubén and I are helping my parents at our family's store. My name is María. My father and mother have owned the store for thirteen years. Before that, it belonged to Mami's mother—my grandmother. The store is our family business.

Mami and Papi sell groceries—mainly fruits and vegetables. Today, they are also selling flowers. Everyone in the neighborhood is buying them!

"May I have a nice bunch of tulips, please?" asks Mr. Marosi.

"Yes," says Mami. "Your mother loves tulips."

I look at the empty tulip pail. "Mami," I say, "the tulips are all sold!"

"Oh, my!" she says.

I look in the other pails of water. The roses are gone. The carnations are gone. "Mami, all the flowers have been sold!"

Mami gives Mr. Marosi some lemonade and then whispers to me. "María, I want you and Rubén to go to your grandmother's house."

"But . . . ," I say.

"Hurry, now," Mami says. "I have an idea."

We hurry out of the store as Mami dials the phone. Abuelita's house is not far away.

"María! Rubén! My two helpers," says Abuelita when we arrive. In no time we have a basket of flowers from her garden.

At the end of the day, we are happy. Mr. Marosi got his tulips, and we have sold almost all the flowers.

"Look, Mami," I say. "I hid the most beautiful bunch for you. Happy Mother's Day!"

"Oh, María! Thank you!" She hugs me and thinks for a moment. "I have another idea," she whispers.

Together we give another beautiful bunch to Abuelita. It is the end of a very good day for our family business.

Related Vocabulary

At the Grocery Store

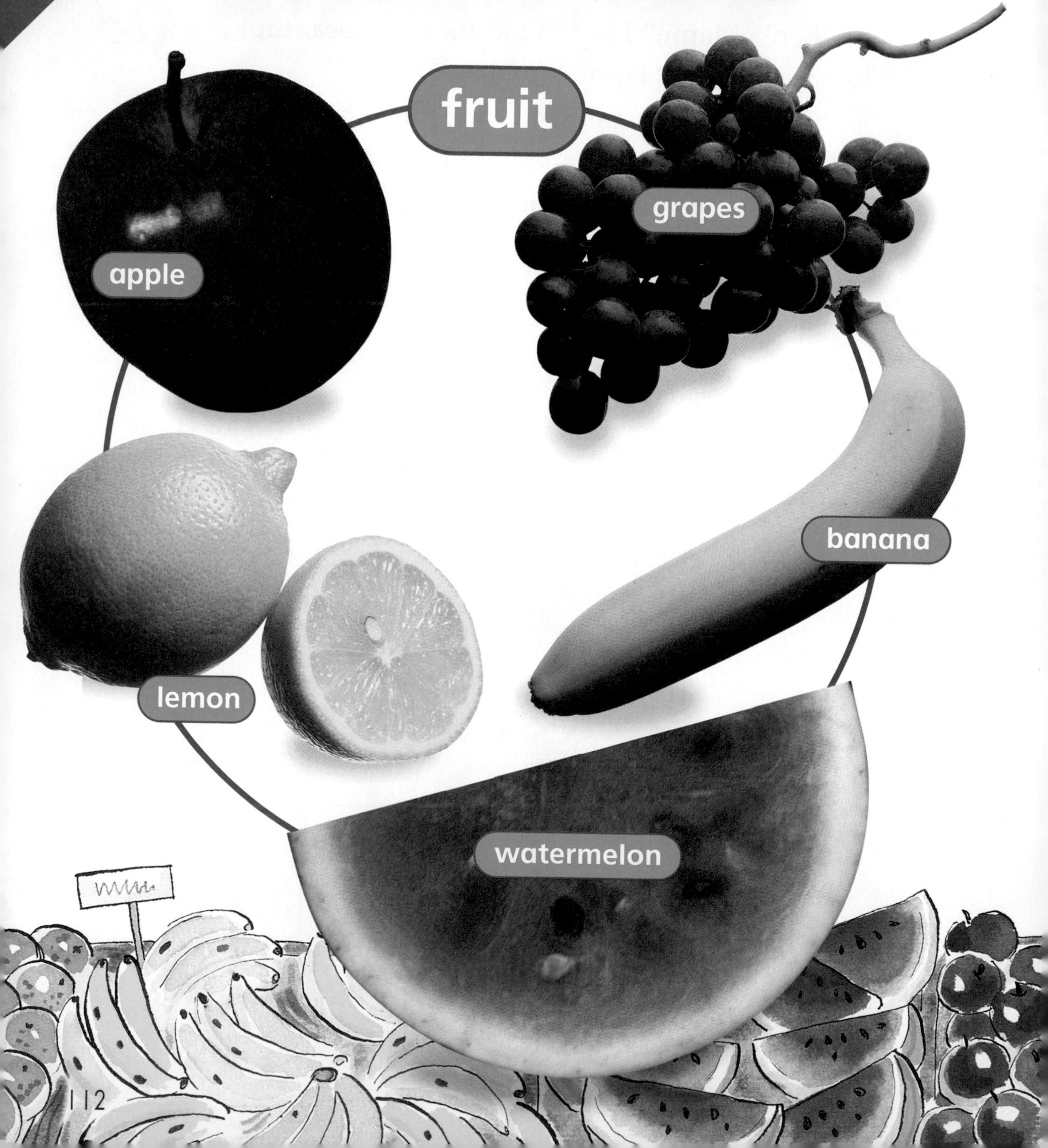
fruit
apple
grapes
banana
lemon
watermelon

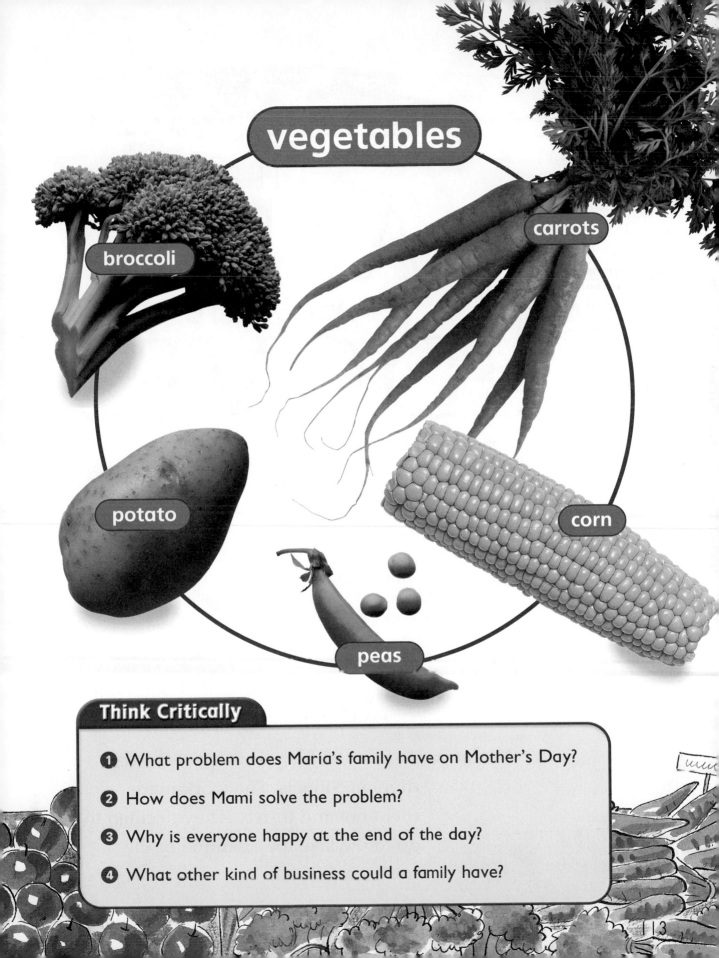

vegetables

broccoli

carrots

potato

corn

peas

Think Critically

① What problem does María's family have on Mother's Day?

② How does Mami solve the problem?

③ Why is everyone happy at the end of the day?

④ What other kind of business could a family have?

Review Vocabulary with a Play

STORIES ON STAGE

THE ANTS AND THE DOVES

AN AESOP'S FABLE

CHARACTERS	SETTING
Narrator	A quiet forest
Roberto, an ant	next to a lake,
Ants	Summer
Elena, a dove	
Doves	
Man	

Narrator: A group of busy ants spent the day digging tunnels. The work made them hot and thirsty. They decided to go to the lake for a sample of the fresh, cool water.

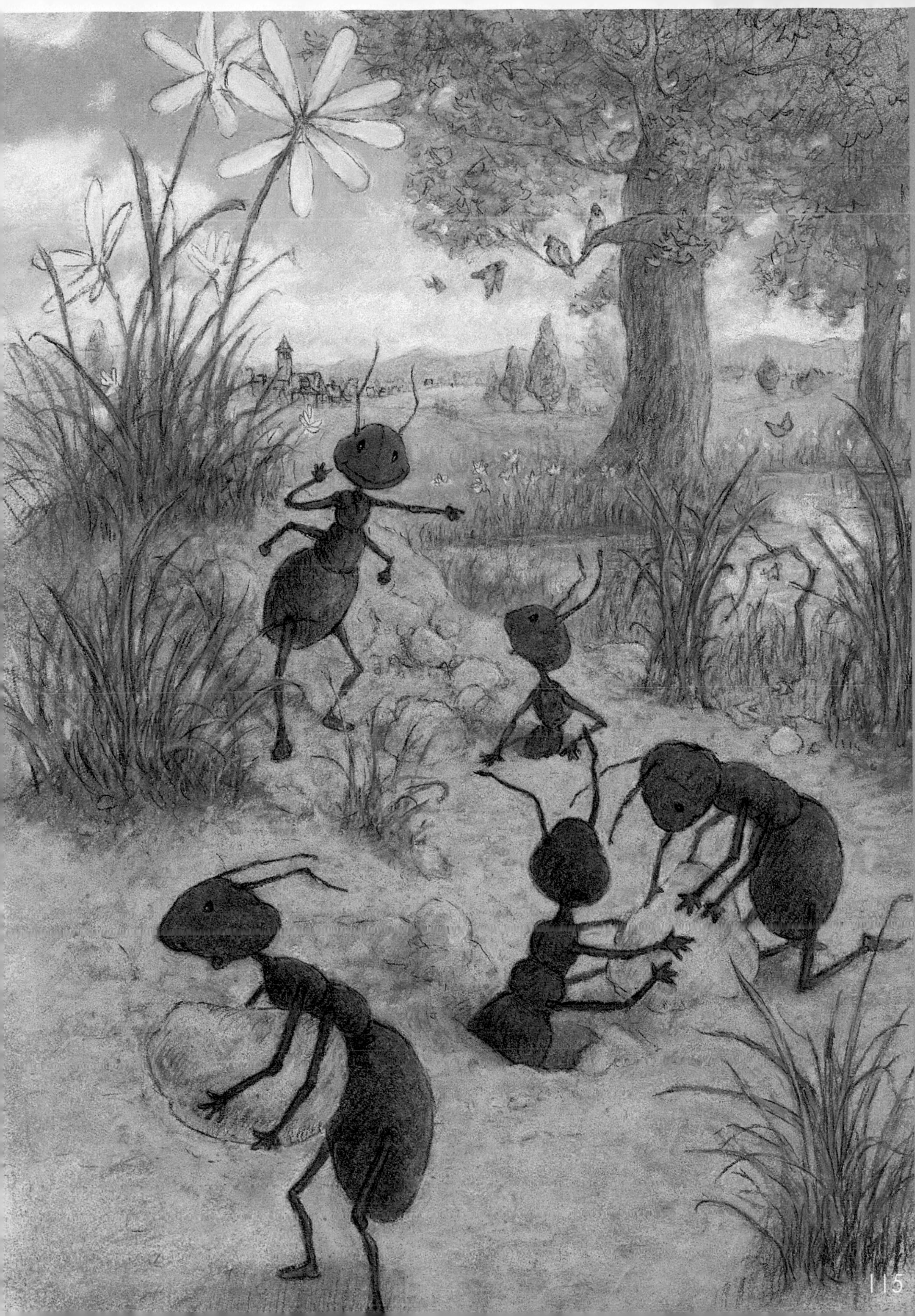

Roberto: Let's walk out to the end of that twig and drink from the lake. We must be careful not to fall in, though.

Ants: Yes, that's a good idea. We need to be careful!

Narrator: The ants worked as a team. Holding on to one another, they walked carefully to the water. Roberto sipped the water and smiled.

Roberto: Ah! This water is cool and tasty.

Ants: Ah! Cool and fresh!

Narrator: All of a sudden, a strong wind blew across the lake. It blew the twig back and forth.

Roberto: Hold on tight! Don't fall into the lake!

Narrator: The wind was so strong that the ants fell into the water.

Roberto and the Ants: Please, somebody help us!

Narrator: The ants were in a lot of trouble! Right next to the lake stood a big tree. In the tree sat some doves. The doves heard the ants' cries for help.

Elena: Look down there at those poor ants! If we don't help them, they might drown!

Narrator: The doves flew to the lake, carrying a small branch.

Elena and the Doves: We're on our way!

Narrator: The doves dropped the branch gently into the water near the ants. The ants climbed onto the branch and rode it safely back to land.

Roberto: Doves, you are all so brave! How can we ever thank you?

Narrator: Some of the ants quickly marched to the garden. They picked the prettiest flowers they could find and brought them back to the doves.

Roberto: Please take these beautiful flowers as a gift. If you ever need anything, we will try our hardest to help you.

Elena: Thank you. Everyone needs help from friends once in a while.

Narrator: A few days later, a man came walking through the forest. He wore heavy gloves and carried a net, which he waved at the doves. As they tried to fly away, one of them was caught in the net.

Elena: Oh, no! What will we do? The man has caught my brother!

Doves: He will try to catch the rest of us, too! What will we do? Help! Help!

Narrator: Down on the ground, the ants heard the doves' cries for help. Roberto pointed to the tree with the doves.

Roberto: Quick! March to the tree. We must help our friends!

Ants: Yes! We must help them!

Narrator: The ants marched to the tree and found the man. They climbed up his boots. Then they climbed up his legs and started to bite. The man jumped and yelled.

Man: Ow! Ow, ow! I've got to get out of here!

Elena and the Doves: He's gone, thanks to you, Ants! You saved us.

Narrator: When friends live close together, they should help each other. The moral of the story is that one good turn deserves another.

Review Activities

Think and Respond

1. Think about the selections you read in this unit. Why is it good to work together?

2. In "Cleaning Bear Lake" and "The Great Big Enormous Rock" a problem is solved. How are the problems alike?

3. In "Ant Cities," how are the ant teams like teams of people? How are they different?

4. In "The Family Business," María helps in her family's store. How do you help your family?

5. How would "The Great Big Enormous Rock" end if the characters did not work together?

LANGUAGE STRUCTURE REVIEW

Describe a Location

Work with a partner. Take turns describing a place you know. Give your partner clues such as

- There is a big door in front.
- Many people work there.
- There are shelves with lots of boxes and canned food.

Create Word Riddles

Take turns creating riddles. Choose a Vocabulary word, and ask your partner questions about it. Your partner has to guess which word you have chosen. For example:

RIDDLE: What begins with *b* and can take you places?

ANSWER: It's a bus!

Play until you have made up riddles for all the Vocabulary words.

butterfly

cactus

jackrabbit

lizard

SING ALONG

Growing Up

Every day
We all grow,
Getting smarter as we go.
Making each skill
Better still
As we work and play
Helps us grow in every way!

*Sing to the tune of
"This Old Man."*

armadillo

Narrative Elements: Plot

The **plot** is what happens in a story. Often, a character in a story has a problem to solve. The story ends once there is a solution to the problem.

Read the story. Think about the problem and the solution. Then look at the chart below.

Amy wished her vegetables would grow. Instead, the soil was dry and her plants were brown.

Then a storm came, and it rained for days. Amy went outside to look at her vegetables. At last, they had grown!

Plot	
Problem:	**Solution:**
Amy's garden will not grow.	It rains, and Amy's garden grows.

Try This

▶ Read the story. Then, on a separate sheet of paper, copy the chart below. Complete the chart using information from the story.

Winter was coming, and Sarah's summer flowers would soon die in the cold. She would miss their bright colors. Then she had an idea.

Sarah saved some seeds from her favorite flower. She dried the seeds and planted them in a pot indoors. The plant would grow inside where it was warm, and she could still enjoy her flowers!

Plot	
Problem:	**Solution:**

Vocabulary POWER

Alamo Across Texas ▼

VOCABULARY

river

water

shade

drought

ocean

exhausted

rain

drifted

We have had no **rain** for weeks. The pond is dry because of the **drought**.

The **river** was wide and blue. Our little boat **drifted** slowly along.

Dad and I were **exhausted** after our long ride. We sat in the **shade** and rested.

The flowers need **water** to grow.

My family runs by the **ocean**.

Alamo
Across Texas

by Jill Stover

On the Lavaca River in the great state of Texas, there once lived an alligator named Alamo. Life along the river suited Alamo perfectly.

He had plenty of water, lots of tasty fishes, a fine shade tree, and an interesting assortment of friends and neighbors.

But one year there came a drought. Day
after day the sun beat down, until there was no
more water, no more tasty fishes, no more
shade tree, and no more friends and neighbors.

Life along the river was no longer pleasant
at all. So Alamo set off down the trail to find a
new home.

He walked and he walked and he walked and
he walked . . .

until he came to a Texas ranch.

The ranch had water . . .

but no tasty fishes, and his new neighbors were
too curious. So Alamo hit the trail again.

He walked and he walked and he walked and
he walked, until he came to the ocean. There
were lots of tasty fishes . . .

but the water was rough and far too salty.
So Alamo hit the trail again.

He walked and he walked and he walked and
he walked, until he came to a swimming pool.
The pool was full of water . . .

but there were no tasty fishes, and it was far
too crowded. So Alamo hit the trail again.

He walked and he walked and he walked and
he walked, until he came to a city.

The city had water *and* fishes, but what a
racket! It didn't smell too good either. So Alamo
hit the trail again.

He walked and he walked and he walked
and he walked and he walked and he walked.
But there was no more water to be found in
the whole state of Texas.

At the end of the trail, exhausted and dry as a bone, Alamo curled up under a cactus and fell asleep.

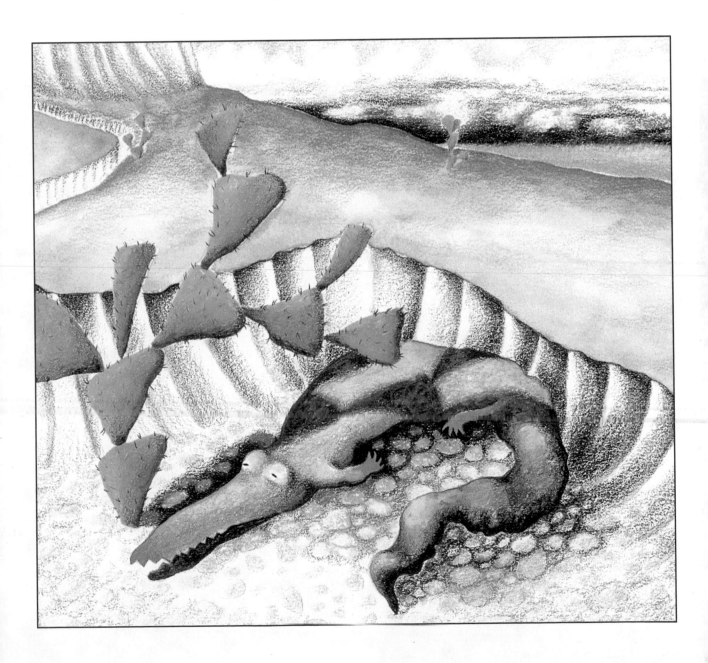

And while Alamo slept, it began to rain at last.

It rained and it rained and it rained and it rained. Fast asleep, Alamo drifted.

And drifted.

In the morning, when he awoke, he could
hardly believe his eyes.
Home!

Think Critically

1 What happens to Alamo's home?

2 Why was life along the river no longer pleasant for Alamo?

3 Why do you think Alamo is exhausted at the end of
the trail?

4 Would you rather live near a river or near the ocean?
Explain.

Vocabulary POWER

From Baby to Adult ▼

VOCABULARY

shaky

strong

grown-up

paws

warm

calf

herd

cub

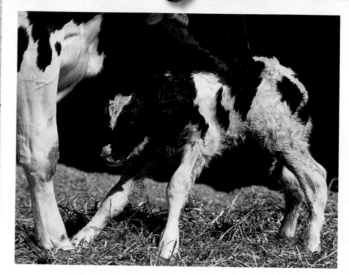

This **calf** is trying to stand, but its legs are **shaky**.

A bear **cub** grows quickly. It will soon be a **grown-up** bear.

A bear has large **paws** and **strong** teeth.

Thick fur keeps polar bears **warm** in winter.

A **herd** of cows grazes on the grass.

From Baby to Adult

You were once a little colt.
Your sister was a filly.
You stood on shaky little legs.
Your first steps looked so silly.
Now you are a tall brown horse,
On legs so strong and fast.
You run across the country fields,
A grown-up horse at last.

foal

You were once a playful pup,
Tugging on my fur.
You ran around the house all day.
How very cute you were!
Now you are a golden dog.
Your puppy days are past.
You walk so nicely on your leash,
A grown-up dog at last.

You were once a baby cat,
A kitten soft and small,
With big, round eyes and mitten paws,
The cutest pet of all.
Now you are a happy cat.
Your kitten days are past.
You like to curl up warm and purr,
A grown-up cat at last.

kangaroo

joey

You were once a small joey.
I carried you so near.
I kept and fed you in my pouch
For most of your first year.
Now you're out and on your own,
Big and strong and fast,
Hopping on your two back legs,
A kangaroo at last.

You were once a little calf,
Staying close to me.
But you grew up fast, and soon
You were roaming free.
Now you travel with the herd
And blow your trumpet call,
A grown-up elephant at last,
The strongest of us all.

calf

bear

cub

You were once a tiny cub.
You played and ate and grew.
I taught you how to hunt and fish.
I took you swimming, too.
Now you're big and powerful.
Your baby days are past.
You wander through the woods alone,
A grown-up bear at last.

elephant

Related Vocabulary

Animal Homes

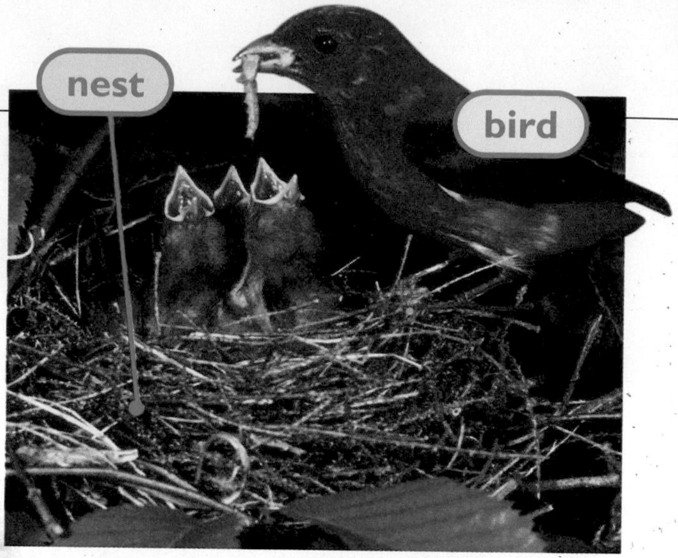
nest
bird

▲ A bird raises its young in a nest.

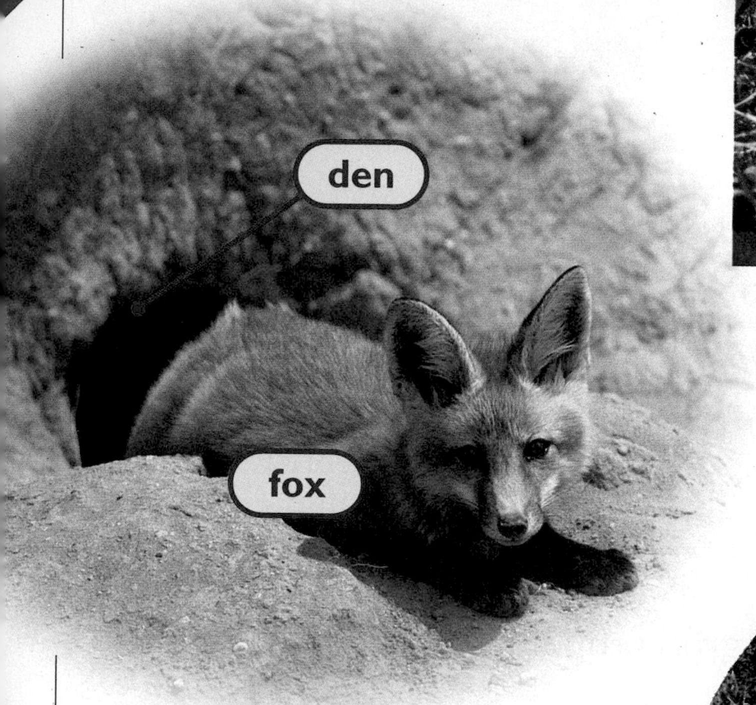
den
fox

▲ This fox's den is an underground burrow.

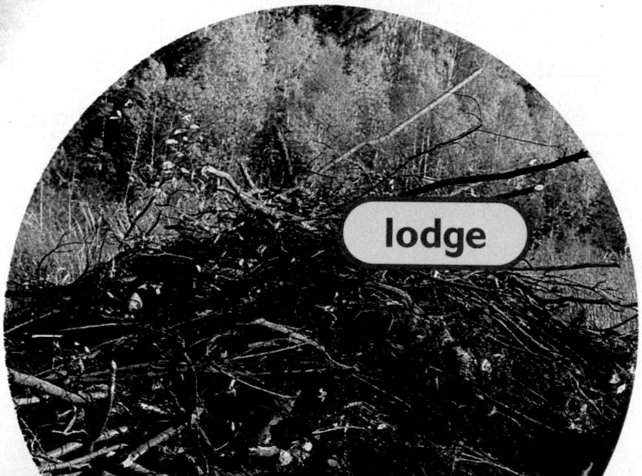
lodge

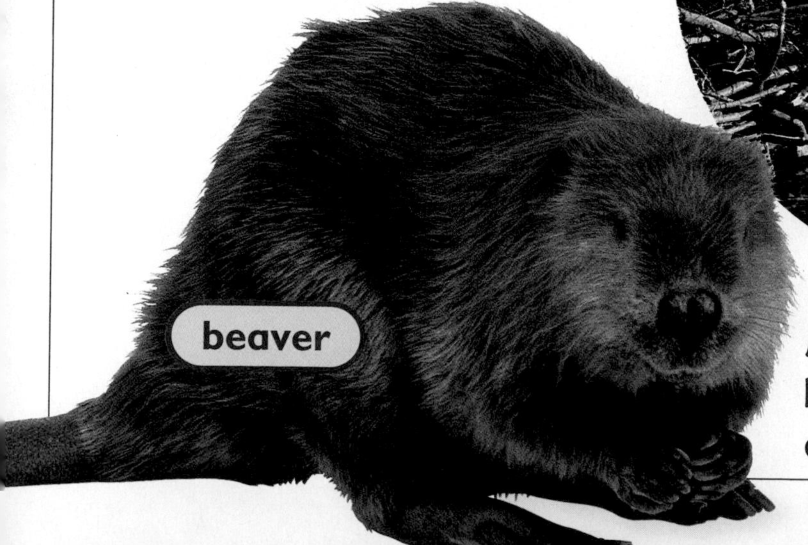
beaver

▲ A beaver builds a lodge from branches of trees.

bees

hive

◄ Bees live and work in a hive.

A prairie dog lives under the ground in a burrow. ▶

prairie dog

burrow

Think Critically

1 How do the animal babies change as they grow up?

2 Who is telling each young animal's story?

3 How does the mother kangaroo take care of her joey?

4 Which animal did you find most interesting to read about? Why?

Vocabulary POWER

Tricks Animals Play ▼

VOCABULARY

enemy

protects

shell

safe

danger

sharp

hide

grass

A bear has long, **sharp** claws.

A white seal uses its color to **hide**. Its **enemy** cannot see it on the snow.

Green bugs can hide in the green **grass**.

A turtle's **shell** is hard. It **protects** the turtle from harm.

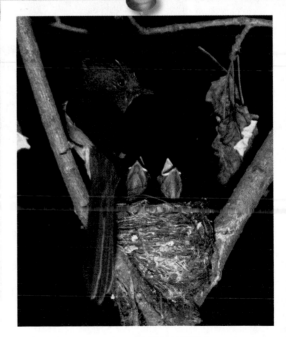

Birds are in **danger** on the ground. They are **safe** up in their nests.

TRICKS ANIMALS PLAY

BY JAN NAGEL CLARKSON

opossum

The Opossum Plays Dead

HISS! The opossum tries to scare an enemy. If the enemy does not go away, the opossum falls down and plays dead. When it lies very still, it is playing possum. Then an enemy may leave it alone. This is a trick that protects the opossum. Other animals have unusual ways to get food and to keep from being eaten.

Turtles Wear Hard Shells

The box turtle has a hard shell. It can pull its head, legs, and tail inside its shell. Then the turtle is as safe and snug as if it were inside a box.

box turtle

shell

These Fish Puff Up Like Balloons

A porcupine fish gulps water when there is danger. It puffs up, and sharp spines stick out all over its body. Do you think another fish will try to swallow a puffed-up porcupine fish?

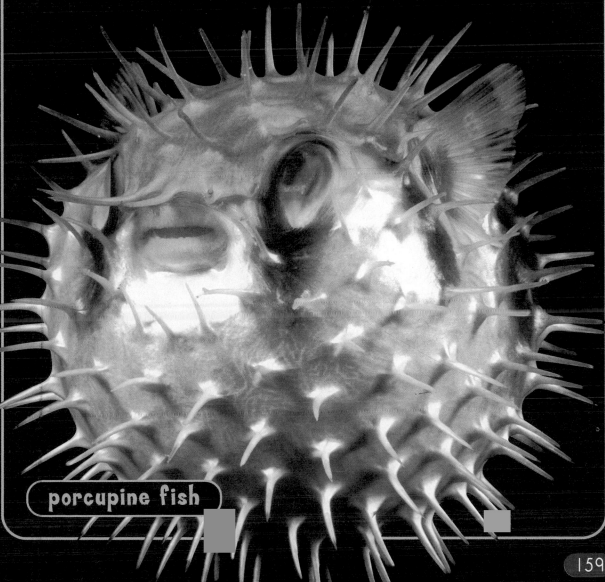

porcupine fish

killdeer

Some Animals Protect Their Babies in Special Ways

The killdeer is a bird that pretends it is hurt to lead an enemy away from its chick. The bird drags one wing as if it were broken. An enemy will follow because a hurt bird is easy to catch. After the bird leads the enemy far away, it flies back to its chick.

These baby fish hide in their mother's mouth.
The mother spits them out when it is safe.

mouthbreeder fish

Some Animals Use Tools

The chimpanzee sticks a blade of grass into a termite nest. Then it eats the termites that bite the grass. The sea otter pounds a clam on a rock to open it.

The grass and rock are tools that help the animals get food. Once people did not believe animals used tools. Don't you think these animals played a good trick on people?

chimpanzee

sea otter

Think Critically

1. How does an opossum protect itself?

2. What does the porcupine fish do when it is in danger?

3. Why does the killdeer pretend to be hurt in front of its enemies?

4. Why do you think animals play "tricks"?

Vocabulary POWER

Homes Around the World ▼

VOCABULARY

weather

houses

different

materials

environment

bricks

tents

float

People live in many kinds of **houses**. These may be very **different** from ones you've seen.

Houseboats are homes that **float** on the water.

Tents are easy to put up and take down.

Houses are made of many **materials**. Some are made of **bricks**, which are very strong.

People use materials from the **environment** to build shelters from the **weather**.

Homes Around the World

by Lucy Floyd

All people need homes to shelter them from the weather. Shelters also provide safety and a place to rest.

Around the world, people build houses of different kinds. What kind of house do you live in?

old-style houses

Houses in different parts of the world are built in many ways to shelter people from the weather.

In cold lands, houses are built to keep out wind and snow. They help people stay warm in winter.

In hot lands, houses are built to keep out the sun and let in a breeze.

chalet

grass house

log cabin

People build shelters out of materials from the environment. They may use trees, branches, mud, rocks, or grass.

Some homes are made from straw. Other shelters are made from blocks of snow!

In the past, people made tepees out of animal skins. Since these people were hunters, they needed homes that were easy to take with them on a hunt.

straw house

igloo

tepee

homes made of stone and brick

adobe house

yurt

Some homes are much like those of the past. In earlier times, people who lived in hot places baked clay bricks in the sun. Then they built houses with the bricks. Today, people make houses of clay bricks with thick walls that keep out the sand and sun.

In the far north, people once made winter homes from blocks of snow. People there now use this kind of shelter only on hunting trips.

Tents are types of shelters that have also been around for years. Some people who live in the sandy desert today still live in tents.

Some people live in homes that float! In some parts of the world, many people live on houseboats.

Many people enjoy living near the water.

houseboat

People who live where river waters rise when it rains build homes on poles above the water. In every part of the world, people love the homes that keep them safe!

stilt houses

Inside an Apartment

living room

lamp

curtains

chair

sofa

rug

bedroom

window

bed

bookcase

closet

kitchen

cabinets

counter

sink

stove

refrigerator

oven

Think Critically

1. What kinds of materials are used for homes built in hot areas?

2. Why do you think people used tepees on hunting trips?

3. How are homes today like homes of the past?

4. What kind of shelter would you build, using the materials around you?

Review Vocabulary with a Play

STORIES ON STAGE

Moving to a New Town

Characters:

Narrator   Mr. Kim

Ellen   Victor

Tanya

Scene 1

NARRATOR: Ellen and Tanya were best friends. They lived right next door to each other. Then one day, Ellen's father got a new job in a new town. Her legs felt shaky when she heard the news. She ran to tell Tanya.

ELLEN: Oh, Tanya! My father says we have to move to another town.

TANYA: It won't be so bad, Ellen. We can talk on the telephone.

ELLEN: I'll have to go to a new school! I won't have any friends! I wish you could come with me, Tanya.

TANYA: You'll make new friends. When I moved to this town, I didn't know anyone. Then I moved next door to you. Look what good friends we are now, Ellen.

NARRATOR: Soon the time came for Ellen to leave. Ellen and Tanya sat in the shade on Tanya's back steps.

TANYA: I have something for you, Ellen. It's a diary. I put a photograph of me on the first page. If you ever feel lonely at your new home, you can look at my picture and write in the diary. It will be just like talking to me.

NARRATOR: The next day, Ellen and her family waved good-bye to the neighbors. Ellen would miss her old house and school, where she felt safe. She would miss Tanya, but she wanted to see her new home, too.

Scene 2

NARRATOR: Ellen liked her new house very much. She decorated her new room and made it feel cozy. The next day would be Ellen's first day at her new school, and she felt a little nervous. She decided to telephone Tanya to tell her how she felt.

ELLEN: Hi, Tanya! Tomorrow is my first day of school. I'm a little scared.

TANYA: Don't worry! Your first day of school will be fun. You'll make a lot of new friends, Ellen.

Ellen: You're right. I'll be okay. I feel better now. When can you visit me, Tanya? I miss you!

Tanya: I already asked Mom. I'll have to wait until the next school vacation.

Ellen: I can't wait to see you!

Tanya: I can't wait to see your new house. Good luck with school tomorrow, Ellen!

Narrator: The next day, Ellen walked into her new classroom.

Mr. Kim: Class, this is Ellen Stone. She is new to our school. Welcome, Ellen!

Narrator: Ellen wished she could hide. It was hard to meet so many different people!

Victor: Hi, Ellen. I'm Victor. I just moved here a few months ago. There are other new students here, too.

Narrator: That night, Ellen felt exhausted from her long day. She curled up in her warm bed and wrote in her diary.

ELLEN: Dear Diary, today was my first day at my new school. I was a little nervous, but I met a new friend named Victor. I guess this school won't be so bad after all.

NARRATOR: The next day, when she got to school, Ellen saw Victor standing outside. It looked like it was about to rain, but he waited for Ellen before going inside.

VICTOR: Hi, Ellen! Hurry so we don't get stuck in this bad weather!

Scene 3

NARRATOR: When school vacation came, Tanya visited. Ellen couldn't wait to show Tanya her new town and have her meet Victor. Ellen and Tanya walked to the playground next to Ellen's home. They met Victor there.

VICTOR: Hi, Ellen. Who is your friend?

ELLEN: This is Tanya. I used to live next door to her before I moved to this town.

VICTOR: Hello, Tanya! It's nice to meet you.

TANYA: See, Ellen? I knew you would be okay in your new town. You've made a very nice friend already!

ELLEN: Tanya, you helped me with the diary and by talking on the telephone. I may have new friends now, but you will always be my best friend!

Review Activities

Think and Respond

1. Tell about two ways people and things grow and change in the selections in this unit.

2. Alamo the Alligator learns that "there's no place like home." What does that mean?

3. How have you changed since you first started school? What is still the same about you?

4. Think about one of the animal tricks you read about. How does it help the animal survive?

5. How do animals choose what home to build?

LANGUAGE STRUCTURE REVIEW

Talk About Likes and Dislikes

With a group of classmates, sit in a circle. To start, one person completes these sentences:

I like _____. I don't like _____.

The next person tells what that person likes and dislikes, and then completes the sentences about his or her own likes and dislikes. For example:

Ana likes ice cream. She doesn't like cake.

I like nature. I don't like noisy places.

VOCABULARY REVIEW

Act Out Words

Choose a Vocabulary word, but don't tell your classmates what it is. Act out the word. If you need more people, ask some classmates to help you.

Your classmates try to guess the word. The classmate who guesses correctly chooses the next word and acts it out.

How can I show the word **grown-up**?

Farmers plant their crops in the **ground** in rows.

It is a little past twelve o'clock. It could be **noon** or midnight.

A **festival** is a time to celebrate. These women **dance** at a festival in Mexico.

This hourglass uses **sand** to measure one hour. When the last **grain** of sand falls, one hour has passed.

The Ant and the Grasshopper

retold and illustrated by Amy Lowry Poole

A long time ago, in the old Summer Palace at the
edge of the Emperor's courtyard, there lived a
grasshopper and a family of ants.

The ants awoke every day before dawn and
began their endless tasks of rebuilding their house of
sand, which had been washed down by the evening
rains, and searching for food, which they would
store beneath the ground.

They carried their loads grain by grain, one by one, back and forth, all day long.

The grasshopper liked to sleep late into the morning, rising as the sun stretched toward noon.

"Silly ants," he would say. "You work too hard. Come follow me into the courtyard, where I will sing and dance for the great Emperor."

The ants kept on working.

"Silly ants," the grasshopper would say. "See the new moon. Feel the summer breeze. Let us go together and watch the Empress and her ladies as they prepare for midsummer's eve."

But the ants ignored the grasshopper and kept on working.

Soon the days grew shorter and the wind brought cooler air from the north. The ants, mindful of the winter to come, worked even harder to secure their home against the impending cold and snow. They foraged for food and brought it back to their nest, saving it for those cold winter months.

"Silly ants," said the grasshopper. "Don't you ever rest? Today is the harvest festival. The Emperor will feast on mooncakes and sweet greens from the fields. I will play my music for him until the moon disappears into the smooth lake water. Come and dance with me."

"You would do well to do as we do," said one of the ants. "Winter is coming soon and food will be hard to find. Snow will cover your house and you will freeze without shelter."

But the grasshopper ignored the ant's advice and continued to play and dance until the small hours of the morning.

Winter arrived a week later and brought whirls of snow and ice. The Emperor and his court left the Summer Palace for their winter home in the great Forbidden City. The ants closed their door against the ice and snow, safe and warm, resting at last after their long days of preparation.

And the grasshopper huddled beneath the palace eaves and rubbed his hands together in a mournful chirp, wishing he had heeded the ant's advice.

The Seasons

Winter

snowman

snow

hat

scarf

boots

mittens

Spring

tee shirt

flowers

seeds

garden

hose

Summer

sun

lifeguard

pool

swimming

goggles

Fall

rake

leaves

basket

pumpkin

Think Critically

1. What does the grasshopper do while the ants work?

2. Why do the ants work so hard?

3. What important lesson does the grasshopper learn at the end of the story?

4. Are you more like an ant or a grasshopper? Explain your answer.

Vocabulary POWER

Stories and Storytellers ▼

VOCABULARY

childhood

tales

fables

grandchildren

favorite

rooster

characters

writer

Mr. Thomas spends each weekend with his **grandchildren**. It is his **favorite** part of the week.

My dad spent his **childhood** on a farm. He had a **rooster** as a pet.

Mrs. Lewis is a **writer**. She likes to write **tales** of adventure.

I like to read **fables**. The **characters** are usually animals who can speak.

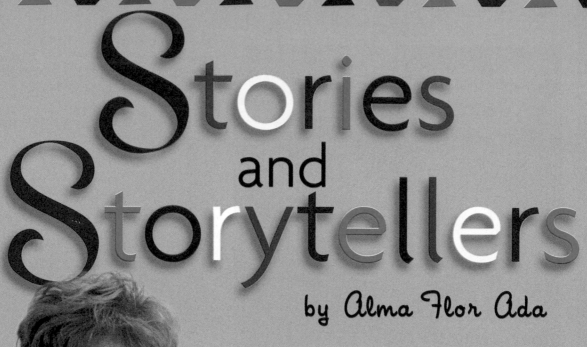

Stories and Storytellers

by Alma Flor Ada

Stories were an important part of my childhood. I lived with my parents, grandparents, uncles, and aunts in a big, old house in Cuba. Everyone around me liked to tell stories, and I loved to listen!

Alma Flor Ada as a child in Cuba.

Alma Flor Ada (left) with members of her family.

Alma Flor Ada enjoys telling stories to her granddaughter, Camila.

My grandmother Lola liked to tell old stories. Sometimes she told me exciting tales about the brave men and women in Cuban history. At other times, she told me fables. These were stories with animals who acted like people. Often the small animals were smarter than the larger ones!

I like to tell old stories, too. Many of them have been passed on from parents to children and from grandparents to grandchildren. When my own children were small, I loved telling them the same stories my grandmother told me. I had learned many lessons from those stories!

Alma Flor Ada likes to write books for others to read.

One of my children's favorite stories was about a rooster who was going to his uncle's wedding. He had forgotten to have breakfast, so he became very hungry along the way. The rooster saw a kernel of corn that was stuck in a puddle of mud. He wanted to eat it, but he knew that it would make his beak muddy. He couldn't go to a wedding with a muddy beak! He had a big decision to make. This story helped my children think carefully about the decisions they made.

My father was also a storyteller. He liked to tell stories about how things came to be. He would start by asking a question. "How did people first learn to cook food?" he once asked me. "Did a hunter drop meat into the fire one night by mistake?" When he saw that I was interested in finding out the answer, he would tell me a story. These stories made me think. It seemed that everything around me had a story!

My uncle Tony told a different kind of story. He liked to tell real-life stories about things that happened in our family. Uncle Tony was always one of the characters— even in the stories that happened before he was born!

The stories I heard as a child have helped me all my life. Now it is my grandchildren's turn to hear some of the stories that have been in my family for so long.

I have written several books about my childhood and the people in my family. I have also written many stories for children. The story of the rooster who went to his uncle's wedding is now a book. Is it a surprise that I became a writer? Stories are all around us. Everyone has a story to tell—even you!

Think Critically

❶ Why is storytelling important to Alma Flor Ada?

❷ How is Alma Flor Ada like the other members of her family?

❸ How were Uncle Tony's stories different from stories told by the author's father and grandmother?

❹ What is your favorite story? Did you hear that story, or did you read it?

Vocabulary POWER

Big Old Bones ▼

VOCABULARY

professor

train

explore

laboratory

giant

lizard

discovery

scientists

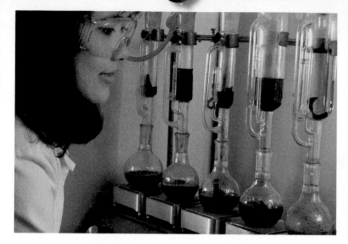

Scientists study things very carefully. They work with special tools in a **laboratory**.

An iguana is a kind of **lizard**. This **giant** lizard can grow up to six feet long.

The group wanted to **explore** the area before going back to camp.

A **professor** spoke to our class about an important **discovery**. A new dinosaur had been found!

My father takes a **train** into the city.

BIG OLD BONES
A DINOSAUR TALE

by Carol Carrick
illustrated by Donald Carrick

In the 1870s, American scientist O.C. Marsh put together pieces of two dinosaur skeletons. One he called apatosaurus and the other he called brontosaurus. Thirty years later, a scientist named Elmer Riggs saw Marsh's mistake. The dinosaur Marsh had named brontosaurus was really another apatosaurus! By then the name brontosaurus was so well known that people used it even though it was wrong.

In the story you are about to read, the main character is Professor Potts. His story is not real, but he makes mistakes just like real people sometimes do.

Long ago, when the Old West was new, Professor Potts and his family were traveling across the country.

Before their train reached the Rocky Mountains, it stopped for water.

209

The Professor was taking a stroll with his family
when their little dog found a bone.

"Very old," said the Professor, examining the bone.
"And very big. I've never seen one like it before."

He decided to stay a few days and explore.

The Professor dug till he had collected a large pile of bones.

And then he took them back East to his laboratory.

LIZARDS
OF THE WORLD

The Professor studied all the books in his
library, but none of them had bones like these.
"Hmm," he said. "It may be some kind of
giant lizard. To know for sure, I'll have to put
the bones together."

First he tried the bones this way.

"The head is too big," said the Professor.

"No one would believe an animal like this."

And too many bones were left over.

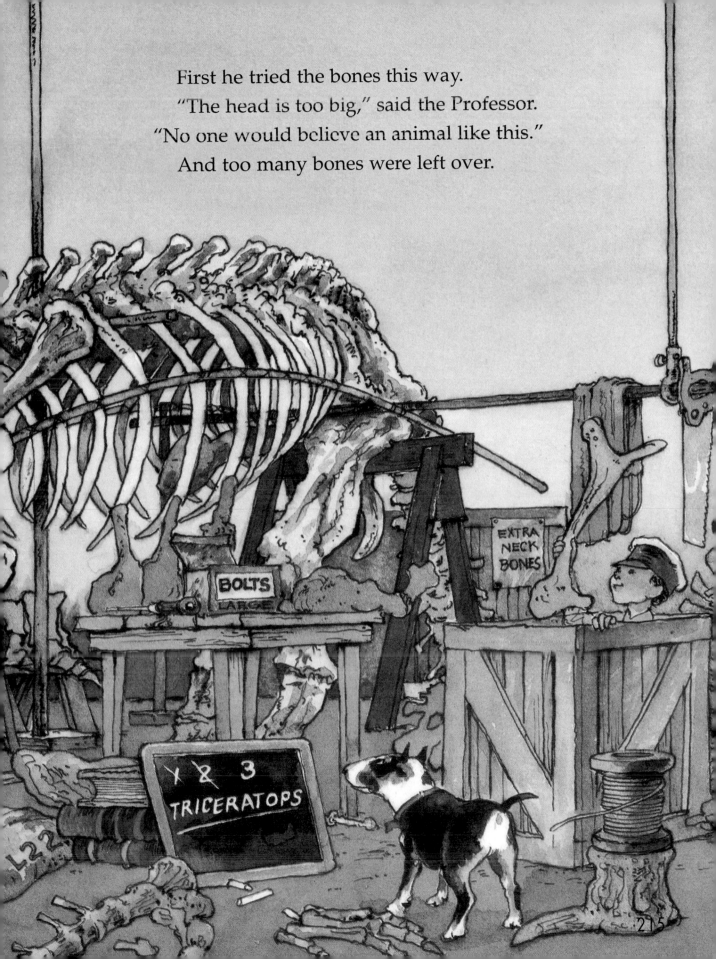

EXTRA NECK BONES

BOLTS LARGE

⅓ × ⅔ 3
TRICERATOPS

Then he tried the bones like this.

The Professor shuddered. "It gives me bad dreams," he said. "Besides, the front legs are too small."

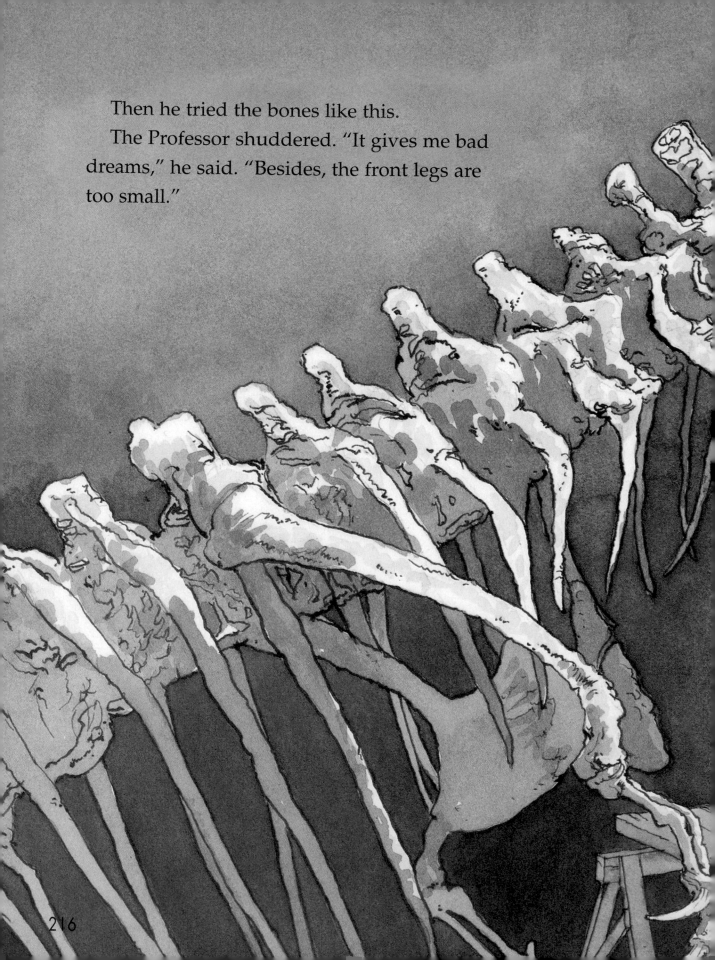

Then the Professor tried the bones
another way.

The neck was so long that he had
to build a bigger laboratory.

"Wrong again," said the
Professor. "An animal this size could
never walk the earth."

BRONTOSAURUS

News spread of Professor Potts's exciting work. Reporters came to his laboratory.

But the Professor was not ready to show them his discovery.

When the strange animal was finally put together, it still didn't look real.

"Bones are only the inside," said the Professor, so he asked his wife to make a skin for it.

At last the great day came when Professor
Potts was ready to share his discovery. Important
scientists arrived from all over the world.

Before he pulled aside the curtain the Professor
made a speech.

"Long ago," he said, "the earth was ruled by a
giant lizard that has never been seen before. I have
named it TRIBRONTOSAURUS REX!"

Everyone pushed forward to get the first look . . .

. . . and they were truly amazed.

28

Think Critically

1. What does Professor Potts do with the bones that his dog finds?

2. How would you describe Professor Potts to a friend? Use examples from the story to explain your answer.

3. How do you know Professor Potts's discovery is important?

4. What discoveries have you made before?

229

Vocabulary POWER

Well, Well, Mr. Bell! ▼

VOCABULARY

inventor

machine

wire

voice

telephone

operator

dial

computers

This is an old **telephone**. It has a **dial** instead of buttons.

Alexander Graham Bell was a famous **inventor**. He made the first telephone.

I asked the **operator** for a telephone number I needed. She spoke with a friendly **voice**.

Many people work with **computers**. The computer is an important **machine** in most offices today.

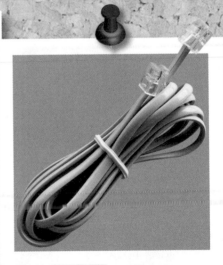

This **wire** will be used to connect the computer to other computers.

Well, Well, Mr. Bell!

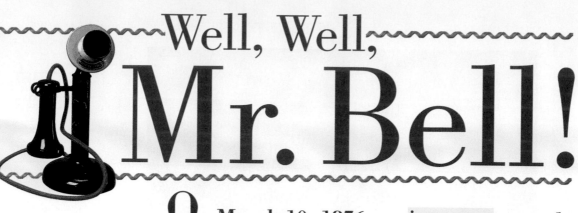

On March 10, 1876, an inventor named Alexander Graham Bell was working in his office. He spoke into a new machine. "Mr. Watson, come here, I want you," he said.

Thomas A. Watson was Bell's helper. He was in another room, working on another machine. A wire connected Bell's machine to Watson's machine. When Bell spoke, Watson heard him on the machine. Bell's voice had traveled over the wire! Alexander Graham Bell had invented the telephone.

Alexander Graham Bell uses his newly invented telephone.

The First Telephones

When Bell and Watson showed what the telephone could do, everyone wanted one. The very next year, the first telephone company was started. Just two years later, 10,000 telephones were being used in the United States!

Workers began stringing telephone wires on poles from city to city. By 1914 telephone wires stretched thousands of miles across the United States. They connected more than one million telephones!

The first telephones were made of wood and metal and had bells on the front.

Operator, Operator!

At first an operator connected all phone calls. When a person picked up the receiver, the operator asked whom he or she wanted to speak with. The operator then plugged in a wire on the switchboard to connect the call. The very first operators were teenage boys, but later on most operators were women.

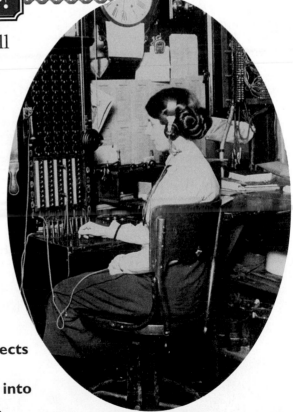

A telephone operator connects phone calls by plugging wires into a switchboard.

Telephones Improve

Telephone companies kept making better telephones. In 1923, the invention of the telephone dial made it possible to make phone calls without an operator. By 1948 telephones were being used around the world—30 million of them!

Phones with dials let people make their calls without talking to an operator.

Connecting the World

In 1956 a ship laid telephone wires under the Atlantic Ocean. Now people in the United States could talk to people in Great Britain. This made it much faster to do business!

Through the Years

In the 1990s, telephones and telephone wires were carrying more than just voices. Computers could send and receive e-mail, or electronic mail. Fax machines could send copies of pages over telephone wires, too.

A fax machine can send a copy of paper to another fax machine.

Telephones continue to change. Now cordless phones and cell phones use radio waves and microwaves to carry voices.

Telephones Today

Today people can use cell phones to make calls as they move around throughout the day. Alexander Graham Bell's telephone has become one of the most important inventions of all time!

This woman talks on her cell phone as she walks through a busy city.

Keeping in Touch

letter

Dear John,
I'm having a great time at my grandparents' house. When I come back home, I'll show you the pictures I took!

Sincerely,
David

mailbox

envelope

e-mail

Plain Memo

Priority File Print Save Delete Encl Clip Spell Receipt Send

FROM: David
TO: John

Hello

Dear John,

I'm having a great time at my grandparents' house. When I come back home, I'll show you the pictures I took!

Sincerely,
David

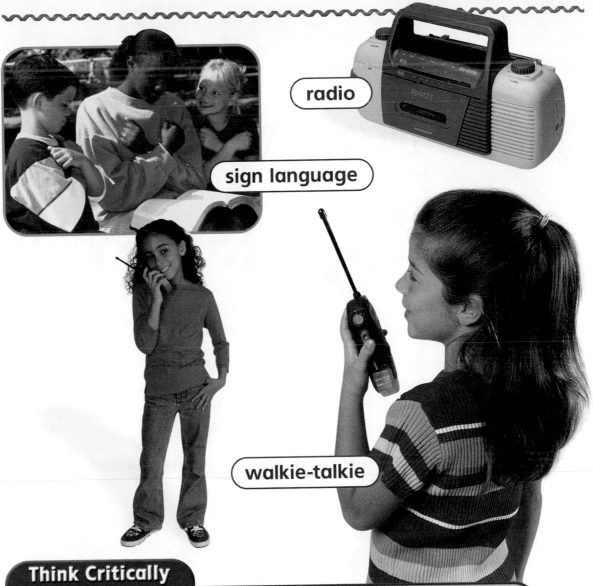

radio

sign language

walkie-talkie

Think Critically

1. How did Alexander Graham Bell's invention change the world?

2. Describe the first telephone operators. Why were they important?

3. How are telephones today different from telephones of the past? How are they the same?

4. Is the telephone important to you? Why or why not?

The Adventures of Pecos Bill

Characters:

Pecos Bill

Coyote

Chuck

Slewfoot Sue

Narrator

Rancher Bob

Scene 1

SETTING: *Along the Pecos River, many, many years ago*

NARRATOR: Pecos Bill lived in Texas a long time ago. People tell many tales about him. When Bill was four years old, he sat crying in the sand on the banks of the Pecos River. A coyote walked up to him to see what was wrong.

COYOTE: Hello, little boy. Are you lost? Don't cry. Come and live with me.

NARRATOR: Bill joined the coyote and her family. As time went on, Bill began to think that he was a coyote, too.

Scene 2

SETTING:	*The banks of the Pecos River, fifteen years later*
NARRATOR:	One day a cowpoke named Chuck found Bill catching frogs by the Pecos River.
CHUCK:	Hello, young feller. My name is Chuck. Can you tell me how to get to El Paso?
NARRATOR:	Suddenly, the biggest rattlesnake in all of Texas slithered out from under a rock!
PECOS BILL:	Chuck, look out!
NARRATOR:	Bill grabbed that giant snake and twirled it in the air like a rope. That's how Bill became the inventor of the lasso.
CHUCK:	Young feller, you saved my life! You are stronger and braver than anyone in Texas. What's your name?
PECOS BILL:	Bill.
CHUCK:	From now on, let's call you Pecos Bill, for the Pecos River. Take this cowpoke hat and these boots, and come with me!
NARRATOR:	Bill said good-bye to his coyote family. He left with Chuck to explore the rest of Texas.

Scene 3

SETTING: *The prairie, two weeks later*

NARRATOR: One day, at around noon, a woman on a horse came up to Pecos Bill and Chuck. She spoke with a voice as big as Texas.

SLEWFOOT SUE: Howdy! My name is Slewfoot Sue! I'm the greatest cowpoke in all of Texas!

PECOS BILL: Howdy! I'm Pecos Bill, and *I'm* the greatest cowpoke in all the West.

CHUCK: As you're both such great cowpokes, come with me. Rancher Bob needs some help.

NARRATOR: Chuck took Bill and Sue to see Rancher Bob. Rancher Bob was trying to catch a calf with a rope.

RANCHER BOB: I can't catch that calf!

NARRATOR: Bill and Sue twirled their lassos and threw them at the calf. Bill caught the calf's neck. Sue caught its legs. Bill and Sue had invented cow roping!

RANCHER BOB: I think you are *both* the best cowpokes in the world!

Scene 4

SETTING: *The prairie, the next April*

NARRATOR: One day, Sue and Bill were playing a game. It was called "What Can You Do?"

SLEWFOOT SUE: Can you use a giant snake as a rope, Pecos Bill?

PECOS BILL: Yep. I'm good at that.

SLEWFOOT SUE: Can you ride a cyclone?

PECOS BILL: A cyclone? That's a tornado!

SLEWFOOT SUE: It's my favorite thing to do.

PECOS BILL: Then I will do it, too, Sue!

NARRATOR: Just then, a big cyclone swept across the prairie. Bill roped that cyclone, pulled it down, and jumped on!

PECOS BILL: Yippee-yi-yay!

NARRATOR: Pecos Bill rode that cyclone all over Texas. He rode it like a big, spinning, flying machine. Slewfoot Sue jumped on the cyclone, too. Bill and Sue rode off into the blue Texas sky to have many more adventures together.

Review Activities

Think and Respond

1. What are some ways people can show creativity?

2. Why do people create and tell fables like "The Ant and the Grasshopper"?

3. What kinds of stories do you like best?

4. How is putting together dinosaur bones creative?

5. Why was the telephone an important invention?

LANGUAGE STRUCTURE REVIEW

Compare Objects

Think of something in the classroom, but don't tell what it is. Describe what you chose by comparing it to other things. For example:

It is smaller than that pencil.

It is bigger than this paper clip.

If no one guesses, let the group ask questions. For example:

Can you write with it?

Play a Word Card Game

You will need two sets of Vocabulary word cards.

- Shuffle the cards. Then lay them face down in rows of six.
- When it is your turn, take two cards. Read the words aloud.
- If the words don't match, put the cards down again exactly where they were. If they do match, use the the word in a sentence.

Wheat is a type of grain.

grain

grain

apartment building

stores

park

248

I like to work after school to earn **money**. My **job** this week is to rake leaves for my neighbor.

I write the new words I learn in my **notebook**.

Tourist
Information
&
Accommodation
Reservations

1

This **banner** tells people where to find information.

Sandy Saves Up

Sandy looked in the window of the bicycle shop on her way home from school. A banner on the front of the shop showed an advertisement for a bicycle she had always wanted. "I wish I could have the shiny purple bicycle in that advertisement," she thought. Summer vacation was near, and she wanted to be able to ride with the neighborhood kids. Sandy decided that she would earn the money to buy the bike.

Sandy knew she would need a job to save up enough money. Maybe she could rake leaves and do other yard work. Or maybe she could walk the neighborhood dogs. She would need all the money she could get to buy that bike before summer vacation.

Sandy's neighbors agreed to pay her to help them with their chores. Every day after school, Sandy walked dogs. Every weekend, she helped her neighbors in their yards. She was very busy!

Now that Sandy was earning money, she needed to keep track of it. She made a budget, or a plan for spending and saving money. She would use this budget to help her manage her money. Then she could save some of it.

In a notebook, Sandy wrote down the amount of money she earned. She also wrote down amounts she received as gifts or allowance. Then she listed the items she bought and how much each item cost.

After several weeks, Sandy checked her budget. She found that she had enough money to buy the bike! Sandy showed her budget and the money to her parents.

Sandy's parents were proud of her for earning enough to buy a bike. "When we go to the bicycle shop," her mother said, "we will buy you a helmet. After all, you must be safe!"

Sandy was looking forward to her summer vacation.

This is the advertisement Sandy saw outside the bicycle shop. Look at the ways advertisements try to persuade people to buy a product.

An **opinion** is something that cannot be proved.

A **fact** is something that can be proved.

257

Saving and Spending

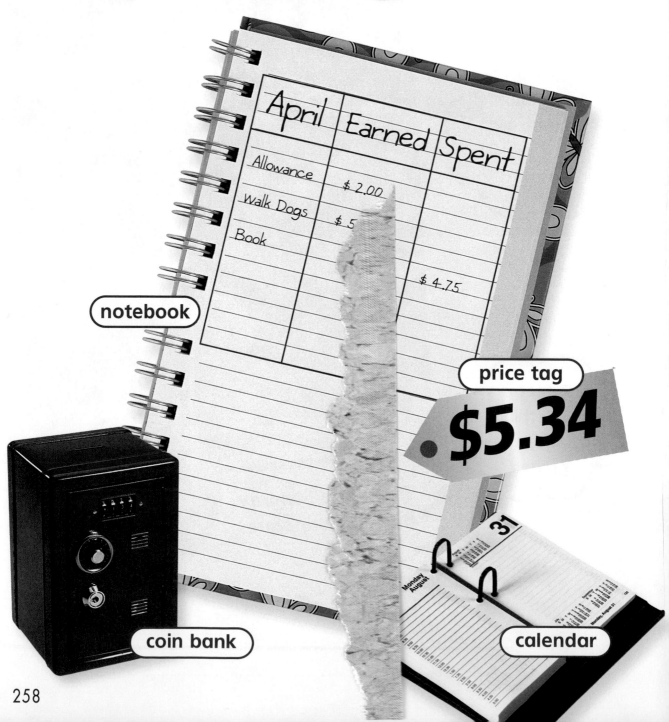

April	Earned	Spent
Allowance	$ 2.00	
Walk Dogs	$ 5	
Book		
		$ 4.75

notebook

price tag

$5.34

coin bank

calendar

BILLS

one dollar

five dollars

ten dollars

COINS

quarter

nickel

penny

dime

coin purse

Think Critically

❶ Why does Sandy need to make money? How does she do this?

❷ How does Sandy keep track of her money?

❸ Why do you think Sandy's parents are proud of her?

❹ Think about an advertisement you have seen lately. What facts and opinions did it use?

Vocabulary POWER

Mr. Santizo's Tasty Treats! ▼

VOCABULARY

baker

proud

orders

ingredients

kitchen

customers

recipe

measures

A **baker** makes breads, pies, and cakes. He is very **proud** of his beautiful cakes.

These **customers** love Mr. Fabio's pizza. He takes their **orders** and gives them the kinds of pizza they ask for.

My parents like to cook together in the **kitchen**. Tonight they are trying a new **recipe** from my mother's cookbook.

Robert's mother puts the **ingredients** for cookies into a bowl. She carefully **measures** each ingredient to get just the right amount.

Mr. Santizo's Tasty Treats!

by Alice K. Flanagan
photographs by Romie Flanagan

Can you smell the hot bread baking and the fresh cookies and apple cakes? Would you like to taste one of the treats that Mr. Santizo makes?

Mr. Santizo is a baker. He is one of the best bakers in the neighborhood.

About fifteen years ago, Mr. Santizo and his wife moved to the United States from Guatemala. Mr. Santizo took a job during the day. At night, he trained to be a baker. Now the Santizos have three children. They are very proud of them.

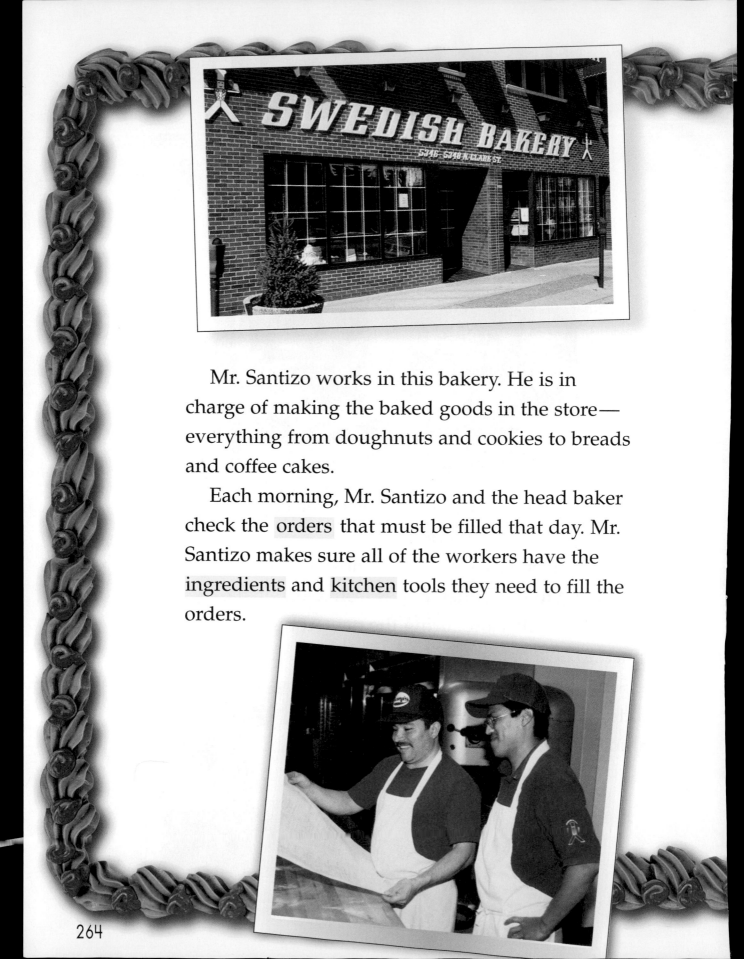

Mr. Santizo works in this bakery. He is in charge of making the baked goods in the store— everything from doughnuts and cookies to breads and coffee cakes.

Each morning, Mr. Santizo and the head baker check the orders that must be filled that day. Mr. Santizo makes sure all of the workers have the ingredients and kitchen tools they need to fill the orders.

Mr. Santizo fills the special orders himself. He makes the cakes and breads that customers order for birthdays, weddings, and special events.

Usually, Mr. Santizo follows a recipe when he bakes. The recipe tells him what to mix together and how much to use.

First he measures the ingredients. Then he mixes them very well. Mr. Santizo is very careful when he uses the fast moving machines, the sharp knives, and the hot ovens.

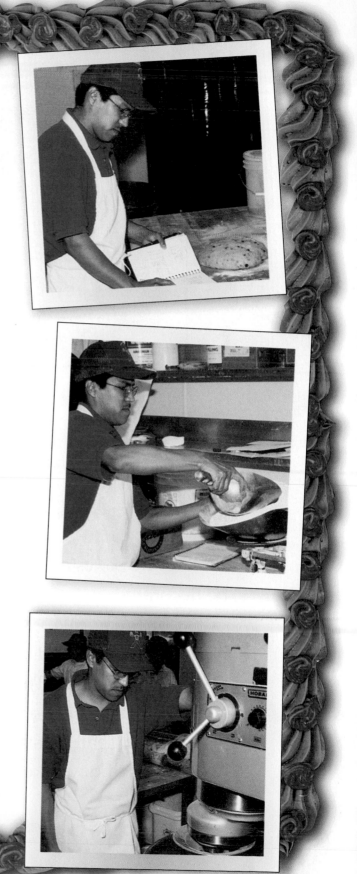

After he bakes and frosts a cake, it's ready to be decorated.

For birthday cakes, Mr. Santizo chooses bright, happy colors. Around each cake, he sprinkles tiny pieces of candy. Then, with steady hands, he makes candy flowers and writes a birthday greeting. Toy balloons add the final touch to a beautiful birthday cake!

Just like an artist, Mr. Santizo creates and decorates wedding cakes. He tries to please his customers by making what they want.

Mr. Santizo feels proud when customers tell him that they like his work. And he listens when they tell him they would like him to make something different for them.

Mr. Santizo likes his job. He does it very well. You can be sure that whatever he makes, it is his very best.

A **jungle** is hot and full of green plants.

Our family went to the beach for our summer **vacation**. We had a great time!

I use **crayons** to draw pictures of **imaginary** animals.

Gloria loves to **paint** pictures. She uses a soft brush to make **smooth** strokes.

The Little Painter of Sabana Grande

by Patricia Maloney Markun

illustrated by Robert Casilla

High in the mountains of Panama lies the village of Sabana Grande. It is very small. Just seven houses of clay adobe stand alongside a brook in a grassy meadow. In the middle house lives the Espino family.

At dawn one cool purple morning, the rooster next door crowed. The Espinos woke up.

Papa went off to the meadow to milk the cow.

Mama stirred up the fire in the open-air kitchen and fried golden breakfast tortillas.

Fernando rolled up his straw sleeping mat and put it in the corner. He hurried to the kitchen to eat his tortilla right away.

This was an important day. At school Fernando had learned to draw colored pictures with crayons. Now school was out for dry-season vacation, and Fernando was going to paint for the first time.

His teacher, Señora Arias, had told him exactly how the country people of Panama made their paints. She said:

"Black from the charcoal of a burned tree stump.
Blue of certain berries that grow deep in the jungle.
Yellow from dried grasses in the meadow.
And red from the clay on the bottom of the brook."

It took him a long time to make the paints. Black was easy, because the burned stump of a big tree lay right next to the Espinos' adobe house.

But Fernando had to look and look before he found those certain berries deep in the jungle, to make the blue paint.

In the corner of the meadow he found a patch of very dry grass, and from that he made a large pot of yellow.

He wandered up and down alongside the brook, looking for clay. The fast-flowing water was too deep for him to reach down to the bottom. At last he came to a bend in the brook where the water was shallow. He reached down and dug up a fistful of clay. It was red, just the way Señora Arias had said.

Now his paints were stirred up and waiting—black, blue, yellow, and red, in four bowls. Next he got out the three paintbrushes his teacher had given him—one very small, one medium-sized, and one especially large.

I'm ready to paint pictures, Fernando said to himself. He picked up the small brush and dipped it into the pot of red. Then he had a terrible thought.

He had nothing to paint a picture on! An artist needs paper.

He looked in both rooms of the house. He could find no paper at all.

He ran from house to house asking everyone in
Sabana Grande for paper to paint on. None of the
neighbors had any. Not a scrap.

Fernando was sad. After all his work he wouldn't
be able to paint pictures—the colored pictures he
could almost see, he wanted to make them so badly.
Paints and brushes weren't enough. He needed
paper, too.

His fingers itched to draw something—anything.
He put down the paintbrush and went over to the
mud by the brook. He picked up a stick and drew in
the wet dirt, the way he had ever since he was a very
little boy.

The big rooster who woke him every morning
came out of the chicken yard next door. Fernando
looked at him and drew the shape of a rooster. He
sighed. He couldn't use his new red and yellow
paints to make a bright rooster. He couldn't make
the rooster's comb red. He could only scratch out a
mud-colored rooster. It wasn't the same as painting
would be. It didn't have any color.

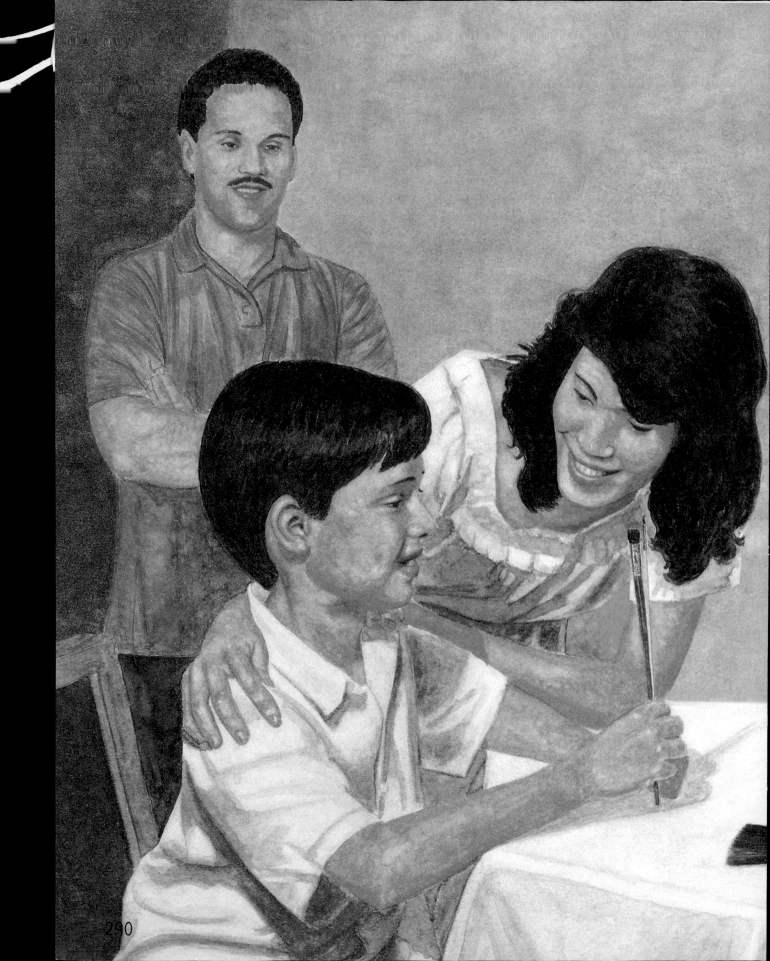

Fernando looked around at the adobe houses of his village. Suddenly he got an idea. Adobe was smooth and white—almost like paper. Why couldn't he paint on the outside of his family's adobe house?

"No!" Papa said. "Who ever saw pictures on the outside of a house?"

"No!" Mama agreed. "What would the neighbors say?"

Fernando looked at his pots of paint and was very unhappy. He wanted to paint pictures more than anything else he could think of.

At last Papa said, "I can't stand to see my boy so miserable. All right, Fernando. Go ahead and paint on the house!"

Mama said, "Do your best, Fernando. Remember, the neighbors will have to look at your pictures for a very long time."

First Fernando made a tiny plan of the pictures he was going to paint, painting it with his smallest brush on one corner of the house.

"Your plan looks good to me, Fernando," Papa said. "If you can paint pictures small, you should be able to paint them big."

Fernando picked up his bigger brushes and started to paint a huge picture of the most beautiful tree in Panama, the flowering poinciana, on the left side of the front door. As he painted, he could look up and see the red flowers of a poinciana tree, just beginning its dry season, blooming on the mountainside.

The neighbors were very surprised.

Señora Endara called out, "Come and see what Fernando is doing!"

Señor Remon said, "Who ever saw a house with pictures on the outside?"

Pepita, the little girl next door, asked, "Does your mother know you're painting on your house?"

Fernando nodded and smiled and kept on painting. Now and then he would look up at the mountain to see the real poinciana. After a week its flowers faded and died. Fernando's tree grew bigger and brighter and redder.

On one branch he added a black toucan with a flat, yellow bill. On another branch a lazy, brown sloth hung by its three toes.

The neighbors brought out chairs. While Fernando worked, they drank coffee and watched him paint.

Next he painted the wall on the other side of the door. An imaginary vine with flat, green leaves and huge, purple blossoms crept up the wall.

Word spread about the little painter of Sabana Grande. Even people from Santa Marta, the village around the mountain, hiked into town to watch him paint. The purple vine now reached almost to the thatched roof.

294

One day Señora Arias came from the school in
Santa Marta. Why was his teacher looking for him,
Fernando wondered. It was still dry season, when
there wasn't any school. It hadn't rained for a month.

"School's not starting yet," his teacher said. "I came
to see your painted adobe house that everyone in
Santa Marta is talking about. Fernando, you did very
well with those paintbrushes. I like it!"

She turned to the neighbors. "Don't you?"

"We certainly do!" the neighbors agreed.

They poured some coffee for the visiting teacher.

"Fernando, will you paint pictures on my house?" asked Señora Alfaro.

"And mine, too?" asked Señor Remon.

Fernando nodded yes, but he kept on painting.

For fun he added a black, white-faced monkey looking down at the people through purple flowers.

Next to the door he painted a big red-and-yellow rooster, flopping its red comb as it crowed a loud "cock-a-doodle-doo!"

Above the door he painted the words CASA FAMILIA ESPINO, so people would know that this was the home of the Espino family.

Now his pictures were finished. Fernando sat down with his teacher and the neighbors. Everyone said kind words about his paintings.

Fernando said nothing. He just smiled and thought to himself, There are still six adobe houses left to paint in Sabana Grande.

Think Critically

1. How does Fernando help his community?

2. Does Fernando paint real animals or imaginary ones?

3. How do you know Fernando's neighbors like his paintings?

4. What part of Fernando's painting do you like best? Tell why.

Review Vocabulary with a Play

★ STORIES ON STAGE ★

Rita Smith, GIRL DETECTIVE

The Case of The Missing Newspapers

Review
VOCABULARY

emergency

shop

village

customers

vacation

notebook

orders

job

bicycle

CHARACTERS:

| Narrator | Rita Smith | Danny Olivera | Mr. Baker | Officer Lee |

SCENE 1

Setting: Rita's front porch, early one Saturday afternoon.

NARRATOR: Rita Smith was sitting on her front porch one day, reading a story. The story was a mystery.

RITA: I love mysteries, so I'm a detective. A detective is a person who solves mysteries. Around here they call me Rita Smith, Girl Detective.

NARRATOR: Danny Olivera came into Rita's yard, looking worried. Usually he had his dog Alfie with him, but this time he was alone.

DANNY: Rita, I need your help!

RITA: What's the emergency? Did you lose Alfie?

DANNY: No. Mom took him to the pet shop to be cleaned up. I'm the one in trouble! All the newspapers I delivered this morning are missing. Now Mr. Baker wants me to pay for them!

NARRATOR: Mr. Baker was Danny's boss. He owned the only book shop in the village.

RITA: Sit down, Danny, and tell me what happened.

DANNY: I delivered the newspapers, the same as always. When I got back home Mr. Baker called me, He was upset because all the customers had called him. No one got a newspaper!

RITA: You left a newspaper at each customer's house?

DANNY: Yes, all but one. Mrs. Arthur is on vacation. I wrote that down in my notebook, where I keep all the orders. See?

RITA: I can see that you take your job seriously. Let's go down to the book shop and look for clues.

Detective for Hire

MYSTERY

SCENE 2

Setting: Mr. Baker's book shop.

NARRATOR: Danny and Rita rode their bicycles to Mr. Baker's book shop. When they got there, Officer Lee was buying a magazine.

RITA: Mr. Baker, did anything unusual happen today? We're looking for clues about the missing newspapers.

MR. BAKER: The only unusual thing was having so many customers call me. No one on your street got a newspaper today.

OFFICER LEE: I got my newspaper this morning. Danny handed it to me as I drove out of my driveway.

DANNY: That's right, I did.

RITA: Did you see anything strange, Officer Lee?

OFFICER LEE: Hmm. No, but I was busy playing with Danny's dog.

RITA: Oh? I thought Alfie stayed at home when you delivered newspapers, Danny.

DANNY: This morning he followed me. I didn't know it until I got to the last house and Officer Lee told me.

RITA: Did you take Alfie right home?

DANNY: I had to. He had black stuff all over his face. He got it all over my shirt, too.

RITA: Where is your shirt now?

DANNY: It's at home. Why?

RITA: I have an idea. Let's go to your house.

SCENE 3

Setting: Danny's house.

NARRATOR: Danny and Rita rode over to Danny's house. They put their bicycles next to Alfie's doghouse.

RITA: Let's go look at the shirt you told me about earlier.

DANNY: Here it is.

RITA: Hmm. I see.

DANNY: Well?

RITA: Are you sure you didn't get your shirt dirty from the newspapers?

DANNY: I'm sure of it. I was wearing a jacket. When I got home, I took it off. That's when Alfie jumped on me and got my shirt dirty.

RITA: Danny, do you have an old newspaper in the house?

DANNY: Yes. Let me get one for you.

RITA: Let's see what happens if I rub it on the shirt. Look at the marks!

DANNY: They're the same as the ones Alfie made!

RITA: Yes! I think I know where we'll find all those newspapers! Come with me.

NARRATOR: Now, where do you think Rita is going? That's right—to the doghouse!

RITA: Well, well, well! There are all your newspapers.

DANNY: That silly dog must have picked them up and taken them home to hide. That's how he got the black stuff on his face!

NARRATOR: That's one more mystery solved by Rita Smith, Girl Detective!

DANNY: I need to deliver these newspapers to my customers again. Thanks, Rita!

RITA: I'm glad I could help.

Review Activities

Think and Respond

1. How are the communities you read about in this unit alike? How are they different?

2. What does Sandy learn by saving for a bike?

3. How is Mr. Santizo like one of the workers in "People Who Help"? How is he different?

4. Choose one of the jobs in "People Who Help." What would a workday on that job be like?

5. How does Fernando help the community of Sabana Grande?

LANGUAGE STRUCTURE REVIEW

Give Commands

Play the game "Simon Says." The leader gives commands such as

Simon says, "Hop on one foot."

Simon says, "Jump three times."

Touch your nose.

Everyone must do what Simon says, except when the leader doesn't say "Simon says." Take turns being the leader.

VOCABULARY REVIEW

Create a Story

Gather the Vocabulary word cards for this unit. Each student takes a word card and stands in a line.

The first student in line begins a story, using the Vocabulary word he or she picked. The next student continues the story, using his or her Vocabulary word. Continue until the last person in line ends the story.

village

bicycle

paint

scuba diver

octopus

shark

SING ALONG

We're Going to Explore!

We're going to explore!
We're heading out the door
To catch a train, a boat, a plane—
To mountain, sea, and shore.

We'll travel far away!
We're heading out today
To go explore the world and more.
We're leaving now! Hurray!

*Sing to the tune of
"The Farmer in the Dell"*

clam

starfish

313

Make Inferences

As you read, you often take clues from the story and add them to what you already know from real life. When you do this, you are **making inferences**.

Read the paragraph below. Think about the clues the author gives you. Then use what you already know to make inferences.

School was over for the summer. Jessica hummed as she packed. She put shorts, shirts, and sandals into her suitcase. At the last minute she remembered her bathing suit.

Story Clues	What I Already Know	My Inferences
Jessica is packing a suitcase.	People take a suitcase when they travel away from home and stay for a while.	Jessica must be going away somewhere for summer vacation.
Jessica packs shorts, shirts, sandals, and a bathing suit.	These are the kinds of clothes people wear in hot weather and for swimming.	Jessica must be going to stay somewhere that is hot and where she can go swimming.

▶ Read the paragraph. Think about the clues the author gives you. Add these clues to what you already know. Then, on a separate sheet of paper, copy the chart below. Use the chart to make inferences about Daniel's grandparents.

For the first time, Daniel's grandparents were coming to visit. Traveling by airplane would be the fastest way to cross the ocean. Daniel wondered how they would like it here, with people speaking English all the time!

Story Clues	What I Already Know	My Inferences

Vocabulary POWER

Beginner's World Atlas ▼

VOCABULARY

maps

locations

overhead

symbols

distance

features

continent

countries

Birds are flying **overhead**. They have flown a long **distance** for the winter.

Some street signs use both **symbols** and words.

LIVING NEAR A VOLCANO

When melted rock pours from a volcano, it is called *lava*. People who live near volcanoes must leave their homes when lava flows toward them. Roads and even houses may be destroyed.

People need to clean up after a volcano erupts. After an eruption, dust covers the land and buildings nearby. *Volcanic dust* is made of tiny pieces of lava. The wind can carry a cloud of volcanic dust around the earth.

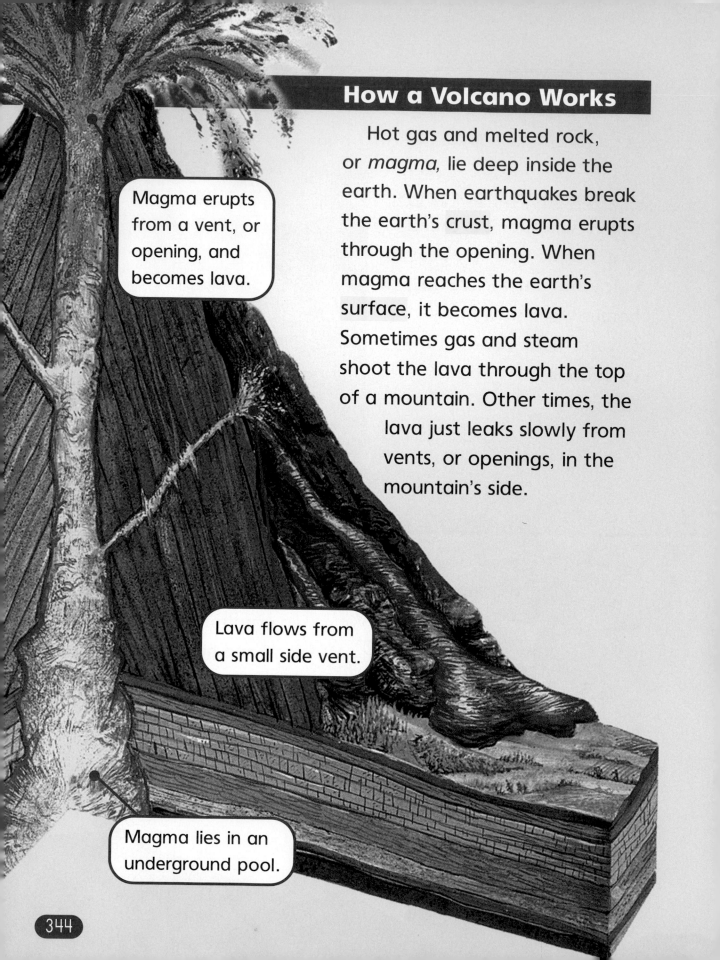

How a Volcano Works

Magma erupts from a vent, or opening, and becomes lava.

Hot gas and melted rock, or *magma,* lie deep inside the earth. When earthquakes break the earth's crust, magma erupts through the opening. When magma reaches the earth's surface, it becomes lava. Sometimes gas and steam shoot the lava through the top of a mountain. Other times, the lava just leaks slowly from vents, or openings, in the mountain's side.

Lava flows from a small side vent.

Magma lies in an underground pool.

TYPES OF VOLCANOES

When some volcanoes erupt, lava spreads widely. New eruptions add layers of lava. This forms a mountain with a gentle slope, called a shield volcano.

shield volcano, ▶ Hawaii

Cinders, or hardened chunks of lava, fly into the air in an eruption. They pile up around the opening, forming a cone-shaped mountain.

◀ Mount Fuji, cone volcano, Japan

WHERE VOLCANOES ERUPT

Many volcanoes are found in a circle around the Pacific Ocean. This is called the *Ring of Fire.* There are also volcanoes in Hawaii, Iceland, and southern Europe.

Many volcanoes are active in the United States. Below is a list of some that erupted between 1900 and 2000.

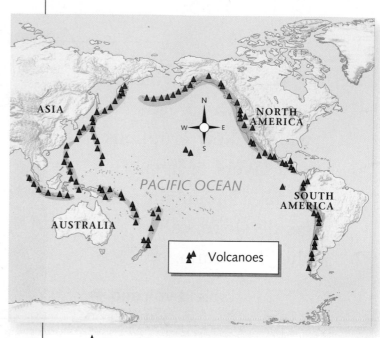

▲ The Ring of Fire circles the Pacific Ocean.

Name and Place	Facts
Katmai Alaska Peninsula	In 1912 erupted more strongly than any other volcano in North America in that century.
Mauna Loa Big Island, Hawaii	World's largest volcano. Erupted 15 times from 1900 to 2000.
Shishaldin Unimak Island, Alaska	Never stops erupting. Sends up smoke and sometimes ash.
Mount St. Helens Washington State	Erupted in 1980, affecting the land for 220 square miles around it.
Kilauea Kilauea, Hawaii	Began to erupt in 1983 and was still active in 2000.

VOLCANOES IN ACTION

On May 8, 1980, the Mount St. Helens volcano in Washington State erupted. Tons of rock slid down the mountain at a speed of 155 miles per hour. The rock slide knocked down 10 million trees. Scientists had told people to leave the area, saving many lives.

Ash covered the land for more than 200 square miles. For a while, no plants or animals could live near the volcano.

Before long, rain and wind made cracks in the hard lava. Seeds landed there and grew, and life returned to the land around Mount St. Helens.

▲ **Mount St. Helens covered in ash**

▲ **New life on Mount St. Helens**

Think Critically

1. How do volcanoes change the earth?

2. What do the words *magma* and *lava* name?

3. How can you tell that volcanoes are powerful?

4. Would you like to live near a volcano? Why or why not?

Vocabulary POWER

Here Comes the Sun ▼

VOCABULARY

star

light

Earth

clouds

raindrops

rainbow

gas

steam

Earth is the third planet from the sun.

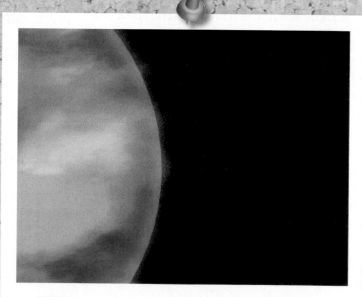

A **star** is a ball of burning **gas**.

Dark **clouds** covered the desert. Then, I felt **raindrops** on my face.

After the rain, the sun's **light** peeked through the clouds. I saw a **rainbow** over the trees.

Hot **steam** shot up from the ground.

Here Comes the Sun

Gifts of the Sun

from Click *magazine*

The Sun is a marvelous star. It gives us heat and light. It causes our weather and seasons. The Sun gives us all the energy we need to live and grow on Earth.

The Sun evaporates water in streams and lakes and oceans to form clouds and bring rain.

When sunlight shines through raindrops, we see a beautiful rainbow.

In spring, the Sun warms our Earth and melts the snow and ice of winter.

351

The Sun's light makes
plants grow. Green plants
soak up energy from the
Sun and turn it into food
we can eat and flowers
we can enjoy. When we
eat fruits and vegetables,
we soak up energy from
the Sun, too!

Energy from the Sun can be used to warm our houses, heat our water, and produce electricity.

From millions of miles away, the Sun shines through the darkness to light up our world!

Every day we wake up and see the Sun.
The Sun is by far the largest object in
the solar system. Nine planets orbit
the Sun, including planet Earth.
Get ready to study the Sun
closely. You might need
your sunglasses!

Sun Boggler
by Catherine Ripley

The Sun is a star.

The Sun doesn't look like the stars you wish upon at night, does it? But it's a star all the same. Just like other stars, the Sun gives off massive amounts of heat and light. Earth, our planet, can't do that. Only a star can. The Sun looks so much bigger and brighter than other stars because it is so much closer to Earth.

The Sun Is HUGE!

Ask your mom or dad if you can count out some frozen or canned peas. Imagine that one pea is Earth. Now count out 108 peas in a line across your kitchen counter or table. (It's easiest if you count out the peas by tens and then line them up.) That's how much wider the Sun is than Earth. In fact, the Sun is so huge that over one million Earths could fit inside it!

Earth

Sun

• = the width of Earth

108 peas

= the width of the Sun

How many groups of 10 peas are needed to make the width of the Sun? Are there any peas left over?

The Sun is a ball of sizzling, bubbling gases.

Most of the Sun is made up of a gas called hydrogen. Have you ever seen a kettle of water boiling? The water inside gets so hot that it changes into steam that puffs out the spout. That steam is called water vapor, which is a gas. Now imagine a giant ball of steaming, storming, spinning gas.

In the very center, or core, of the Sun, the hydrogen gas is so squeezed together and so hot that it changes into another gas called helium. Each second of every day, huge amounts of hydrogen blast into helium. And each time this happens, some extra energy is left over. Slowly, over millions of years, this extra energy pushes out to the surface of the Sun. Then it streams out into space, mainly as heat and light. This sunlight and warmth reaches all the way to us on Earth!

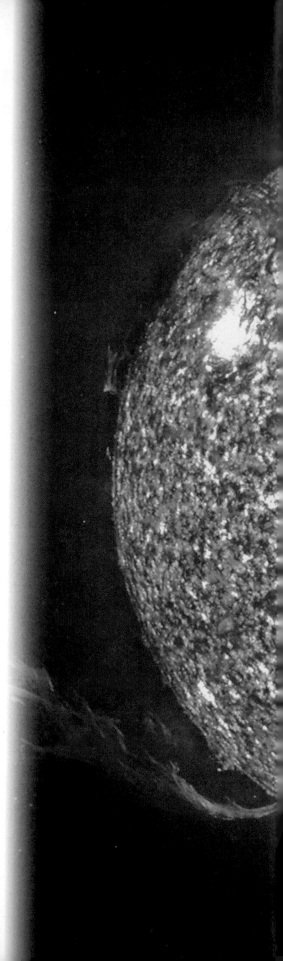

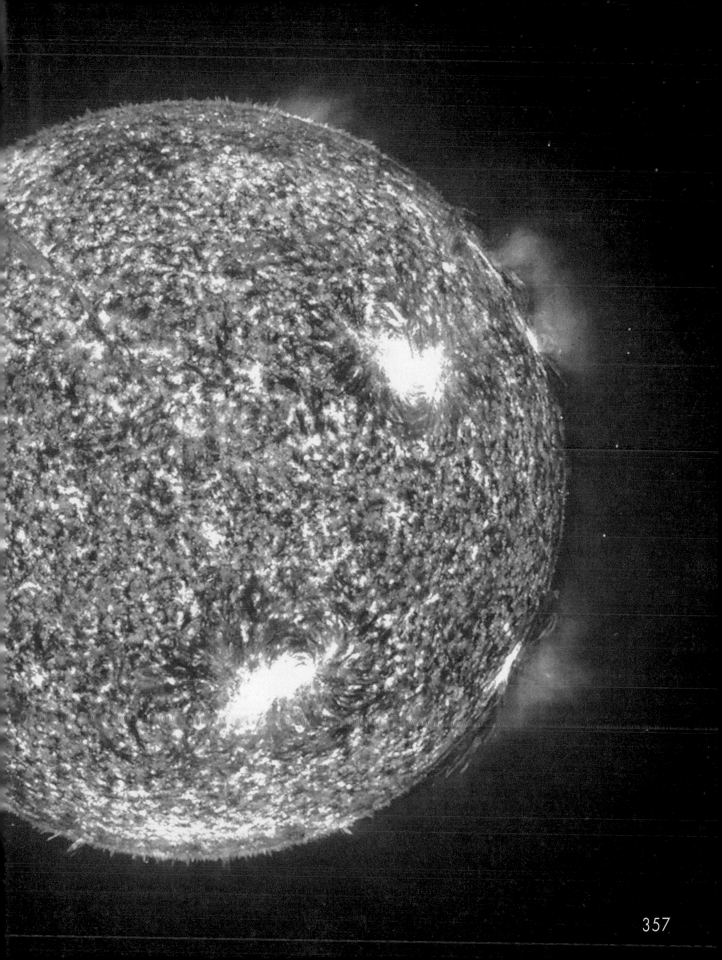

357

The Solar System

Pluto

Neptune

Uranus

Saturn

Jupiter

It takes about 28 days for the moon to orbit Earth one time. This is about as long as one month.

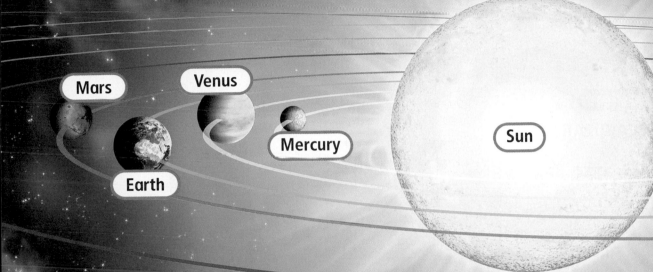

Mars

Venus

Earth

Mercury

Sun

Think Critically

1 What does the Sun do for us?

2 How do you know the Sun is bigger than Earth?

3 How would our world be different without the Sun?

4 What is the most interesting fact you learned in this selection?

Review Vocabulary with a Play

STORIES ON STAGE

Journey to the North Pole

Characters

Narrator

Store Owner

Robert Peary

Matthew Henson

NARRATOR: For many years, no American dared to explore the frozen northern region of Earth. Finally, a group of explorers decided that they would face the ice and cold to find the North Pole. These explorers were led by two men named Robert Peary and Matthew Henson. Peary and Henson knew they would make a good team from the moment they met.

SCENE 1

Setting: Washington, D.C., 1887

STORE OWNER: May I help you, sir?

PEARY: Yes. My name is Robert Peary. I need some supplies for my next trip. I was hoping you might help me.

STORE OWNER: Robert Peary? You're the famous explorer! I know another explorer. He works for me here at the store. His name is Matthew Henson. Let me introduce you to him.

HENSON: How do you do? I'm so glad to meet you.

PEARY: It's nice to meet you, too, Matthew. I hear you like to explore.

HENSON: Yes. I love exploring! When I was twelve years old, I traveled around the world.

PEARY: I have been looking for someone to join my team. What are some of your skills?

HENSON: I am good at reading maps and charts.

PEARY: Would you like to join us? We're going to Central America soon. If we work well together there, we can explore other locations in the future.

HENSON: I would love to join you!

NARRATOR: Henson's skills and bravery made him an important member of the team. After exploring Central America for two years, Peary decided to travel to the North Pole.

363

SCENE 2

Setting: the Arctic, 1908

NARRATOR: Peary and Henson tried to reach the North Pole six times. It was not an easy journey!

PEARY: So many things have kept us from reaching the North Pole! We've run out of food. The ice and snow are dangerous. I'm getting tired of trying.

HENSON: We can't give up. With each try we've learned more about the Arctic. We've learned how to speak the language of the people who live here. They've taught us how to survive in the freezing weather. I'm sure we'll reach the North Pole. Grab those lanterns, Robert! We have some exploring to do!

NARRATOR: Peary and Henson decided that they would try one more time to reach the North Pole. Five other teams joined their team. They started for the North Pole on dog sleds. They would travel a distance of more than 400 miles on this journey!

PEARY: Matthew, I think we should split up the team. You and three others will go with me.

HENSON: Men, this will be a dangerous journey. The crust of ice could break under us. We must be careful, but we can do it. Let's go, team!

NARRATOR: The sun's light on the surface of the snow was blinding. Big pieces of ice stood like sculptures. The explorers raced toward the North Pole. They were sure they would reach it this time! Suddenly Peary stopped.

PEARY: Matthew, you and the rest of the team go on ahead. My feet are frozen, and I can't walk.

HENSON: Don't worry, Robert! You can ride on the sled. You've made it this far. We can't go on without you!

NARRATOR: After a long, icy journey, the team made it to the North Pole. The explorers were tired, but they were excited. They had reached their goal!

HENSON: We're here! We finally made it!

NARRATOR: Henson stuck an American flag into the ice, and he and Peary shook hands.

PEARY: I couldn't have done it without you, my friend. You are one of the greatest explorers in the world!

HENSON: I couldn't have done it without you, either!

NARRATOR: Soon newspapers all over the United States reported the news of the team's great discovery. To this day, Robert Peary and Matthew Henson are known as two of the world's greatest explorers.

Review Activities

Think and Respond

1. Which place that you read about in this unit would you most like to explore? Why?

2. How would a world map or an atlas help you read "The World Celebrates"?

3. What events do people in other countries celebrate? How are some of these events alike?

4. What words can describe both the sun and a volcano?

5. Why is the sun so important to life on Earth?

LANGUAGE STRUCTURE REVIEW

Share Feelings and Ideas

With a partner, review each selection in this unit. Take turns completing some or all of these sentences:

I liked this selection because

_____.

This selection made me feel

_____.

After reading this selection, I think _____.

> After reading this selection, I think I want to be an explorer.

Create Word Categories

Sort the Vocabulary into categories such as

- Words About Nature
- Words About Maps
- Other Words

Then work in a group to discuss how each person sorted the words. If some words were sorted differently, what were the reasons? Could some words fit in more than one category?

Nature	Maps	Other
clouds		delicious

Using the Glossary

A glossary is like a dictionary. It lists words in alphabetical order. To find a word, look it up by its first letter or letters.

To save time, use the **guide words.** They are at the top of each page. They show you the first and last words on the page. Look at the guide words to see if your word comes between them in the alphabet.

Here is an example of a glossary entry:

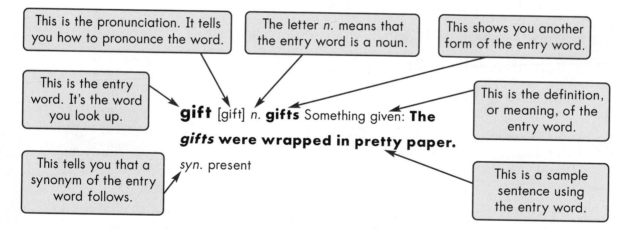

This is the pronunciation. It tells you how to pronounce the word.

The letter *n.* means that the entry word is a noun.

This shows you another form of the entry word.

This is the entry word. It's the word you look up.

gift [gift] *n.* **gifts** Something given: **The gifts were wrapped in pretty paper.**

syn. present

This is the definition, or meaning, of the entry word.

This is a sample sentence using the entry word.

This tells you that a synonym of the entry word follows.

Word Origins

Sometimes an entry word is followed by a note about the word's origin, or beginning. The note tells you what the word first meant and how it has changed. Words often have interesting backgrounds that can help you remember what they mean.

Here is an example of a word origin note:

harvest Until the eighteenth century, *harvest* named the season we now call *autumn.* That was the time when many crops were picked.

Pronunciation

The pronunciation is in brackets that look like this [ ]. The pronunciation is a respelling of the entry word that shows how the word is pronounced.

This **pronunciation key** tells you what the symbols in a respelling mean.

Pronunciation Key*

a	add, map	m	move, seem	u	up, done
ā	ace, rate	n	nice, tin	û(r)	burn, term
â(r)	care, air	ng	ring, song	yo͞o	fuse, few
ä	palm, father	o	odd, hot	v	vain, eve
b	bat, rub	ō	open, so	w	win, away
ch	check, catch	ô	order, jaw	y	yet, yearn
d	dog, rod	oi	oil, boy	z	zest, muse
e	end, pet	ou	pout, now	zh	vision, pleasure
ē	equal, tree	o͝o	took, full	ə	the schwa, an
f	fit, half	o͞o	pool, food		unstressed vowel
g	go, log	p	pit, stop		representing the
h	hope, hate	r	run, poor		sound spelled
i	it, give	s	see, pass		*a* in *above*
ī	ice, write	sh	sure, rush		*e* in *sicken*
j	joy, ledge	t	talk, sit		*i* in *possible*
k	cool, take	th	thin, both		*o* in *melon*
l	look, rule	t̲h	this, bathe		*u* in *circus*

Other symbols
- • separates words into syllables
- ˈ indicates heavier stress on a syllable
- ´ indicates light stress on a syllable

Abbreviations: *adj.* adjective, *adv.* adverb, *conj.* conjunction, *interj.* interjection, *n.* noun, *prep.* preposition, *pron.* pronoun, *syn.* synonym, *v.* verb

*The Pronunciation Key and adapted entries that appear on the following pages are reprinted from *HBJ School Dictionary*. Copyright © 1990 by Harcourt, Inc. Reprinted by permission of Harcourt, Inc.

A

a•dult [ə•dult′ *or* ad′ult] *n.* **a•dults** A fully grown person or animal: **Tadpoles turn into frogs as *adults*.**

ad•ver•tise•ment [ad′vər•tīz′mənt *or* ad•vûr′tis•mənt] *n.* A message that tries to sell you something: **Katie read an *advertisement* for toys on sale.**

advertisement

an•i•mal [an′ə•məl] *n.* **an•i•mals** Anything alive that is not a plant: **Some *animals* are pets.**

B

ba•by [bā′bē] *n.* **ba•bies** A very young child: **The *babies* were learning to walk.**

baby

bak•er [bā′kər] *n.* A person who has the job of baking: **The *baker* used flour to make bread.**

ban•ner [ban′ər] *n.* A piece of cloth or paper with a message written on it: **The *banner* on the front of the store said "Sale Today."**

base•ball [bās′bôl′] *n.* A game played by hitting a ball with a bat: **I got a new bat to use for playing *baseball*.**

bas•ket [bas′kit] *n.* A container made of wood or grass: **Mary sent a *basket* of fruit as a gift.**

bi•cy•cle [bī′sik•əl] *n.* A machine with two wheels, a handlebar, and pedals: **Henry rides his *bicycle* to school.**

basket

break [brāk] *v.* To crack something open or into pieces: **Please *break* the eggs into a bowl.**

brick [brik] *n.* **bricks** A block used for building: **The house is made of red *bricks*.**

brick

broth•er [bruᵵʜ′ər] *n.* **broth•ers** A boy with the same parents as another child: **The two *brothers* bought their mother a gift.**

bus [bus] *n.* A long vehicle in which many people can ride: **The children rode in the school *bus*.**

bus•y [biz′ē] *adj.* Filled with activity: **John works at a *busy* store.**

C

calf [kaf] *n.* The young of the cow, elephant, whale, and some other animals: **The elephants made a circle to keep the *calf* safe.**

can•dle [kan′dəl] *n.* **can•dles** A stick of wax that burns: **Eight *candles* are on the birthday cake.**

catch [kach] *v.* To get hold of something that has been moving: **Hold your hands up to *catch* the ball.**

cel•e•brate [sel′ə•brāt′] *v.* To honor a special event: **Americans *celebrate* the Fourth of July, the day the United States began.**

char•ac•ter [kar′ik•tər] *n.* **char•ac•ters** A person or an animal in a story: **The *characters* in the story were a boy and a dog.**

child•hood [chīld′hŏŏd′] *n.* The time when a person is young: **Mama told funny stories about her *childhood*.**

city [sit′ē] *n.* A large town: **Dallas is a *city* in Texas.**

clip•board [klip′bôrd′] *n.* A board with a clip to hold papers: **Use a *clipboard* to take notes on the field trip.**

clock [klok] *n.* An object that shows the time: **My alarm *clock* wakes me up every morning.**

cloud [kloud] *n.* **clouds** A white or gray shape in the sky: **The *clouds* are white and fluffy today.**

coast [kōst] *n.* The land next to the sea: **There are many lighthouses on the *coast* of Maine.**

com•put•er [kəm•pyo͞o′tər] *n.* **com•put•ers** A machine that helps people work with numbers, words, pictures, and sounds: **Many people use *computers* to write and solve math problems.**

con•ti•nent [kon′tə•nənt] *n.* One of the main land areas on the earth: **North America is a *continent.***

continent

coun•try [kun′trē] *n.* **coun•tries** A place with its own people and government: **The United States is one of the *countries* in North America.**

court•yard [kôrt′yärd′] *n.* An outdoor space with walls on all sides: **The neighbors held a party in the *courtyard.***

cray•on [krā′on *or* krā′ən] *n.* **cray•ons** A stick of colored wax used for drawing: **Melinda drew a tree, using green and brown *crayons.***

Word Origins
crayon The word *crayon* comes from the French word for *pencil*, which at first meant "little chalk."

crayon

crop [krop] *n.* A plant grown on a farm: **Wheat is a *crop* grown in much of the world.**

crop

cross•ing guard [krôs′ing gärd] *n.* **cross•ing guards** A person who stops traffic to help others cross the street safely: ***Crossing guards* stop cars so children can cross the street.**

crust [krust] *n.* The solid outside part of the earth: **The earth's *crust* lies under land and water.**

cub [kub] *n.* The young of the bear, lion, wolf, and some other animals: **The bear *cub* stayed close to its mother.**

cus•tom•er [kus′təm•ər] *n.* **cus•tom•ers** A person who buys something: **Many *customers* bought flowers at the shop.**

dam•age [dam′ij] *v.* **dam•aged** To break or spoil something: **Strong winds *damaged* the roof.**

dance [dans] *v.* To move the body to music: **Max liked to *dance* to the drums.**

dance

dan•ger [dān′jər] *n.* Something that may cause harm: **People face *danger* when they cross busy streets.**

de•li•cious [di•lish′əs] *adj.* Very good to taste: **Everybody wanted more of the *delicious* pie.**

des•sert [di•zûrt′] *n.* A sweet food eaten at the end of a meal: **Have a dish of ice cream for *dessert*.**

dessert

de•stroy [di•stroi′] *v.* **de•stroyed** To ruin completely: **Heavy mud slid down the hill and *destroyed* the houses in its path.**

di•al [dī′əl] *n.* A wheel on older telephones that was used to select the numbers to make a call: **Telephones now have buttons instead of a *dial*.**

dif•fer•ent [dif′rənt] *adj.* Not the same; not alike: **My home is *different* from yours.**

dis•cov•er•y [dis•kuv′ər•ē] *n.* The finding of something that has never been seen before: **The *discovery* of a new planet was big news.**

dis•tance [dis′təns] *n.* The space between two things: **The *distance* between the two towns is about fifty miles.**

drift [drift] *v.* **drift•ed** To float along in water or air: **The empty boat *drifted* down the river.**

drought [drout] *n.* A time when there is very little rain: **Green plants turned brown because of the *drought*.**

dust [dust] *n.* Tiny bits of dirt: **Use a rag to wipe the *dust* off the table.**

Earth [ûrth] *n.* The planet on which we live: **Earth is the third planet from the sun.** *also* **earth:** **Water covers most of the *earth*.**

Earth

egg [eg] *n.* **eggs** A small shell with a baby animal in it: **The bird's *eggs* may hatch soon.**

egg

e•mer•gen•cy [i•mûr′jən•sē] *n.* A sudden event that needs action right away: **Make a plan for getting out of the house if there is a fire or other *emergency*.**

en•e•my [en′ə•mē] *n.* A living thing that may hurt another living thing: **A cat is the *enemy* of a mouse.**

en•vi•ron•ment [in•vī′rən•mənt] *n.* The area in which a person or animal lives: **People who live in a cold *environment* build houses that will keep them warm.**

e•quip•ment [i•kwip′mənt] *n.* Things needed for a special use: **Put this camping *equipment* in your backpack.**

ex•haust•ed [ig•zôst′id] *adj.* Very tired: **We were *exhausted* from the long hike.**

ex•plore [ik•splôr′] *v.* To travel through a place to learn what it is like: **The visitors wanted to *explore* the cave.**

fa•ble [fā′bəl] *n.* **fa•bles** A short story that teaches a lesson: **There are many *fables* about tricky foxes.**

fa•vor•ite [fā′vər•it] *adj.* Best-liked: **Carmen's *favorite* color is red.**

feast [fēst] *n.* A special meal with much food: **Americans have a *feast* on the holiday of Thanksgiving.**

fea•ture [fē′chər] *n.* **fea•tures** A part of something: **Mountains and forests are two *features* of the land.**

fes•ti•val [fes′tə•vəl] *n.* A holiday; a time for feasts and celebrating: **Every fall, the town holds a *festival* with music and dancing.**

fil•ter [fil′tər] *n.* A piece of cloth or paper used to remove dirt from water: **We poured water through a *filter* into a jar.**

fire•fight•er [fīr′fī′tər] *n.* **fire•fight•ers** A person whose job is to put out fires: ***Firefighters* rushed to the burning building.**

fire•works [fīr′wûrks′] *n. pl.* Small rockets that explode with a loud noise and display colored sparks: **Everyone watched the *fireworks* on the Fourth of July.**

firefighter

float [flōt] *v.* To rest on top of the water: **I hope my toy boat will *float*.**

flow•er [flou′ər] *n.* **flow•ers** The colorful part of a plant that makes the seeds: **Petunias and daisies are *flowers*.**

flower

friend [frend] *n.* **friends** Someone you like and who likes you: **The *friends* played together every day.**

fun [fun] *n.* A good time: **We had *fun* at the park.**

gar•den [gär′dən] *n.* a plot of land where flowers, vegetables, and other plants are grown: **Susan helped her grandmother water the *garden*.**

gas [gas] *n.* Something very light that can fill a space but not be seen: **Water can change into a *gas* called water vapor.**

gi•ant [jī′ənt] *adj.* Very large: **The *giant* watermelon was the biggest I had seen.** *syn.* huge

gift [gift] *n.* **gifts** Something given: **The *gifts* were wrapped in pretty paper.** *syn.* present

gift

glove [gluv] *n.* **gloves** A covering for the hand: **The children wore *gloves* to keep their hands warm.**

glove

grain [grān] *n.* A small bit of something: **A *grain* of sand is tiny.**

grand•chil•dren [grand′chil′drən *or* gran′chil′drən] *n. pl.* The children of one's child or children: **Mr. Mendez has two grown children and six *grandchildren*.**

grass [gras] *n.* A green plant with narrow leaves: **The *grass* on the lawn was just cut.**

gro•cer•ies [grō′sər•ēz *or* grōs′rēz] *n. pl.* The foods and other things people buy to meet their needs: **Our family buys *groceries* once a week.**

groceries

ground [ground] *n.* The solid part of the earth's surface: **The roots of plants are under the ground.** *syn.* land

grown-up [grōn′up′] *adj.* Fully grown: **A grown-up bird may look different from its babies.**

har•vest [här′vist] *n.* The gathering of crops: **The corn is tall and ready for the harvest.**

Word Origins

harvest Until the eighteenth century, *harvest* named the season we now call *autumn*. That was the time when many crops were picked.

hel•met [hel′mit] *n.* A hard hat worn to protect the head from injury: **Every bike rider should wear a helmet.**

helmet

herd [hûrd] *n.* A large group of animals of the same kind: **A herd of cows ate grass in the field.**

hide [hīd] *v.* To stay out of sight: **To play the game, everyone tries to hide where no one will look.**

high•way [hī′wā′] *n.* A main road: **Cars can go faster on the highway than on a city street.**

highway

hill [hil] *n.* A part of the land that rises above the land around it: **The ants made a tiny hill of sand.**

hill

hos•pi•tal [hos′pə•təl] *n.* A place where sick people are cared for: **Doctors work at a hospital.**

house [hous] *n.* **hous•es** A building for people to live in: **These houses were built for big families.**

im•ag•i•nar•y [i•maj′ə•ner′ē] *adj.* Made up in the mind and not real: **Alex drew a picture of an imaginary animal with six heads.**

in•gre•di•ent [in•grē′dē•ənt] *n.* **in•gre•di•ents** Something used to make a food: **Sugar and flour are ingredients in cookies.**

in•vent•or [in•ven′tər] *n.* A person who makes something that has never been made before: **The inventor Garrett Morgan made the first traffic light.**

is•land [ī′lənd] *n.* Land with water all around it: **Take a boat to get to the island.**

job [job] *n.* Work that is done to make money: **Armand got a job fixing cars.**

jump [jump] *v.* To spring up from the ground: **I can jump very high!**

jun•gle [jung′gəl] *n.* A thick forest in warm, wet lands: **Monkeys live in the jungle.**

kitch•en [kich′ən] *n.* A room where food is prepared and cooked: **The dishes are in the kitchen.**

lab•o•ra•tor•y [lab′rə•tôr′ē] *n.* A place where scientists make tests: **The water was tested in a *laboratory* to find out what was in it.**

laboratory

lan•tern [lan′tərn] *n.* **lan•terns** A case for a light with openings through which light can be seen: ***Lanterns* help people see in the dark.**

large [lärj] *adj.* Big in size: **Whales can be very *large*.**

late [lāt] *adj.* appearing or coming after the expected time; tardy: **If you don't catch the bus on time, you will be *late* for school.**

laugh [laf] *v.* **laugh•ing** To make a sound to show happy feelings: **We were *laughing* at the funny TV show.**

lay•er [lā′ər] *n.* **lay•ers** A thickness or covering: **Several *layers* of ice covered the lake.**

lem•on•ade [lem′ən•ād′] *n.* A drink made of lemon juice, sugar, and water: **A glass of cold *lemonade* tastes good on a hot day.**

li•brar•i•an [lī•brâr′ē•ən] *n.* **li•brar•i•ans** A person in charge of a library: ***Librarians* help you find books and information.**

light [līt] *n.* A form of energy that we can see: **The sun and electric bulbs give off *light*.**

light

liz•ard [liz′ərd] *n.* A kind of reptile that has four legs and a long tail: **A *lizard* ran out from under a rock.**

lizard

lo•ca•tion [lo•kā′shən] *n.* **lo•ca•tions** The place where something is: **The map shows the *locations* of all the state parks.**

long [lông] *adj.* Having a large distance from end to end: **Ten people sat at the *long* table.**

ma•chine [mə•shēn′] *n.* Something made by people to do work for them: **An exercise *machine* helps a person stay in shape.**

map [map] *n.* **maps** A drawing that shows where things are: **Some *maps* show city streets.**

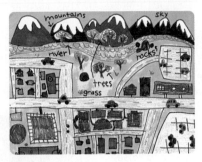
map

ma•te•ri•al [mə•tir′ē•əl] *n.* **ma•te•ri•als** The stuff of which a thing is made: **Wood and stone were the *materials* used to build the house.**

mead•ow [med′ō] *n.* Open land where grass and wildflowers grow: **Sheep ate the grass in the *meadow*.**

meas•ure [mezh′ər] *v.* **meas•ures** To find the exact amount or size of something: **A baker *measures* sugar in a marked cup.**

mon•ey [mun′ē] *n.* Coins and paper bills made by a government and used to pay for things: **Ramona has *money* to buy ice cream today.**

money

moun•tain [moun′tən] *n.* An area of land much higher than a hill: **The top of the *mountain* was white with snow.**

mountain

neigh•bor•hood [nā′bər•hŏŏd′] *n.* An area of a city or town: **There are many children in our *neighborhood*.**

nest [nest] *n.* A place where insects and other animals live and raise their young: **The birds made their *nest* in the old tree.**

nest

new [nōō or nyōō] *adj.* Made or found a short time ago; having been in a place only a short time: **A *new* family moved next door.**

news•pa•per [nōōz′pā′pər or nyōōz′pā′pər] *n.* **news•pa•pers** Several folded sheets of paper with news stories on them: **Mr. Sams reads two *newspapers* every day.**

noon [nōōn] *n.* Twelve o'clock in the daytime: **The sun is high in the sky at *noon*.**

note•book [nōt′bŏŏk′] *n.* A book with lines for writing: **A *notebook* is a good place to write down story ideas.**

notebook

o•cean [ō′shən] *n.* The great area of salt water that covers most of the earth: **Whales swim in the *ocean*.**

op•er•a•tor [op′ə•rā′tər] *n.* A person who runs a machine: **Long ago, telephone calls were made with the help of an *operator*.**

or•der [ôr′dər] *n.* **or•ders** A request to buy or sell something: **The baker received *orders* for ten cakes.**

o•ver•head [ō′vər•hed′] *adv.* Above one's head or in the sky: **Everyone looked up as the plane flew *overhead*.**

paint [pānt] *v.* To make pictures with colored liquids called paints: **Dora used red, yellow, and orange to *paint* a sunset.**

paint

paw [pô] *n.* **paws** The foot of certain kinds of animals: **Cats walk quietly on their soft *paws*.**

peo•ple [pē′pəl] *n. pl.* Men, women, and children: **Many *people* live in the city.**

pic•nic [pik′nik] *n.* An outdoor meal: **We had a *picnic* on the grass.**

picnic

plas•tic [plas′tik] *adj.* Made of plastic, a human-made material: **Plastic bottles do not break.**

po•lice of•fi•cer [pə•lēs′ ôf′ə•sər] *n.* **po•lice of•fi•cers** A person whose job is to protect people: *Police officers* protect us from danger.

pro•fess•or [prə•fes′ər] *n.* A college teacher: **The** *professor* **taught American history.**

pro•tect [prə•tekt′] *v.* **pro•tects** To keep safe from harm: **A crab's shell** *protects* **it from enemies.**

proud [proud] *adj.* Having good feelings about yourself for something you have done: **Manny was** *proud* **that he made a perfect score on the spelling test.**

push [poŏsh] *v.* To press against something to make it move: **Pull the door to get in, and** *push* **it to get out.**

rain [rān] *v.* To fall from the clouds as drops of water: **The clouds turned gray, and it began to** *rain.*

rain•bow [rān′bō′] *n.* Bands of colored light sometimes seen in the sky after rain: **After the rain, a beautiful** *rainbow* **stretched across the sky.**

rainbow

Word Origins
rainbow A rainbow has the same curved shape as a *bow,* used to shoot arrows. The word *rainbow* comes from Old English.

rain•drop [rān′drop′] *n.* **rain•drops** A drop of rain: **Large** *raindrops* **fell on the sidewalk.**

rec•i•pe [res′ə•pē] *n.* A plan for cooking something to eat: **The cookbook has a** *recipe* **for soup.**

ripe [rīp] *adj.* Ready to be eaten: **We picked** *ripe* **apples and ate them.**

ripe

riv•er [riv′ər] *n.* A big stream of water: **Boats sailed down the** *river* **to the sea.**

rock [rok] *n.* A hard object in the earth: **The children sat on the big** *rock.*

roost•er [roos′tər] *n.* A grown-up male chicken: **A** *rooster* **lives with the hens.**

rooster

rope [rōp] *n.* **ropes** A thick, strong cord: **Turn these** *ropes* **for the children to jump.**

run [run] *v.* To move with fast steps: **Jo will** *run* **in the race.**

safe [sāf] *adj.* Free from danger: **You will be** *safe* **if you stay indoors during the storm.**

safe•ty [sāf′tē] *n.* Freedom from danger: **Please read the rules for** *safety* **at the pool.**

sam•ple [sam′pəl] *n.* A small part of something: **We filled a jar with a** *sample* **of the water.**

sand [sand] *n.* Tiny pieces of broken rocks: **At the beach, Juan likes to play in the** *sand.*

sand

school [skool] *n.* A place where people learn: **The children learned to read at** *school.*

sci•en•tist [sī′ən•tist] *n.* **sci•en•tists** A person whose job is to learn more about science: **Space** *scientists* **study stars.**

sculp•ture [skulp′chər] *n.* **sculp•tures** A work of art made out of clay, stone, metal, or other materials: **The *sculptures* of birds were made of clay.**

seed [sēd] *n.* **seeds** The small part of a plant from which new plants grow: **We plant *seeds* in our garden in spring.**

seed

shade [shād] *n.* The shadow of a tree or building: **The dog sat in the *shade* of the tree, where it was cooler.**

shak•y [shā′kē] *adj.* Not strong: **The tiny puppy stood on *shaky* legs.** *syn.* weak

sharp [shärp] *adj.* Coming to a point that can cut: **Watch out for the *sharp* nail!**

sharp

shell [shel] *n.* A hard covering: **A turtle can pull its head into its *shell*.**

shell

shel•ter [shel′tər] *n.* A place where things are safe from weather or danger: **The bear used a cave as a *shelter* for the winter.**

shop [shop] *n.* A place where things are sold: **The *shop* on First Street sells cards and gifts.** *syn.* store

sign [sīn] *n.* **signs** A board with a message on it: **The *signs* on a road tell drivers how fast they can go.**

sign

sing [sing] *v.* **sing•ing** To use the voice to make music: **Everyone was *singing* "Happy Birthday."**

sis•ter [sis′tər] *n.* **sis•ters** A girl with the same parents as another child: **Val is the oldest of three *sisters*.**

smooth [smōŏth] *adj.* Having a surface without any bumps: **The top of the table feels *smooth*.**

star [stär] *n.* A large ball of burning gases in space far from Earth: **The light from a *star* in the night sky travels millions of miles to reach us.**

steam [stēm] *n.* The white cloud that we see as water is changed into a gas by boiling: **A cloud of *steam* came from the teakettle.**

steam

store [stôr] *n.* A building in which things are sold: **We sell fruit at our *store*.** *syn.* shop

stretch [strech] *v.* **stretch•es** To spread out a part of the body: **The runner *stretches* her legs before the race.**

strong [strông] *adj.* Having a lot of power: **A horse runs on *strong* legs.**

sur•face [sûr′fis] *n.* The outside or top part of something: **The *surface* of the road is bumpy.**

sym•bol [sim′bəl] *n.* **sym•bols** A mark or sign that stands for something else: **On a map, circles are often *symbols* for cities and towns.**

tale [tāl] *n.* **tales** A true or made-up story: **I like to read *tales* of adventure.**

teach•er [tēch′ər] *n.* A person who helps others learn: **Our *teacher* showed us how to write a letter.**

team [tēm] *n.* A group of people who work or play together: **A baseball *team* has nine players.**

tel•e•phone [tel′ə•fōn′] *n.* A machine that lets people talk to each other over wires: **The friends talk on the *telephone* every day.**

telephone

Word Origins
telephone The word *telephone* comes from two Greek word parts: *tele* ("far off") and *phone* ("sound, voice").

tent [tent] *n.* **tents** A shelter made of cloth or skin, held up by poles and ropes: **The campers slept in *tents*.**

throw [thrō] *v.* To make something fly through the air: **Eddie can *throw* the ball far.**

tent

to•geth•er [tə•ge_th_′ər] *adv.* With each other: **The children play well *together*.**

train [trān] *n.* A line of railroad cars: **Ms. Lam rides the *train* to her job.**

truck [truk] *n.* A vehicle used to carry loads: **The *truck* brings food to stores.**

truck

tun•nel [tun′əl] *n.* **tun•nels** A path that runs below the ground: **Prairie dogs dig miles of *tunnels*.**

va•ca•tion [vā•kā′shən] *n.* A time when people do not work or go to school: **The children visited the zoo during their *vacation*.**

veg•e•ta•ble [vej′tə•bəl] *n.* **veg•e•ta•bles** A plant or part of a plant that can be used as food: **Corn and carrots are *vegetables*.**

vil•lage [vil′ij] *n.* A small community in the country: **Juan was the first person from his *village* to visit the city.**

vegetable

voice [vois] *n.* The sound made when you talk or sing: **Carlos spoke in a loud *voice*.**

warm [wôrm] *adj.* Having just enough heat but not too much: **The air feels nice and *warm* today.**

watch [woch] *v.* To look at: **I like to sit by the pond to *watch* the ducks.**

381

wa•ter [wô′tər *or* wot′ər] *n.*
A kind of liquid that people,
animals, and plants need to live:
Drink *water* on a hot day.

water

weath•er [weŧh′ər] *n.* What the
air outside is like: **The *weather*
today is cold and cloudy.**

wire [wīr] *n.* A long, thin piece
of metal: **Electricity runs
through a *wire*.**

wire

work [wûrk] *n.* A job: **Each ant has *work* to do.**

writ•er [rī′tər] *n.* A person who writes; an
author: **The *writer* worked for a long time to
finish her story.**

Index of Titles and Authors

Acknowledgments

For permission to reprint copyrighted material, grateful acknowledgment is made to the following sources:

Children's Press/Franklin Watts, a division of Scholastic Inc.: *Mr. Santizo's Tasty Treats!* by Alice K. Flanagan, photographs by Romie Flanagan. Text © 1998 by Alice K. Flanagan and Romie Flanagan; photographs © by Romie Flanagan.

Clarion Books: *Big Old Bones: A Dinosaur Tale* by Carol Carrick, illustrated by Donald Carrick. Text copyright © 1989 by Carol Carrick; illustrations copyright © 1989 by Donald Carrick.

Click Magazine: "Sun Boggler" by Catherine Ripley from *Click* Magazine, Vol. 5, No. 1. Text © 2001 by Catherine Ripley. "Gifts of the Sun" from *Click* Magazine, Vol. 5, No. 1. Text copyright © 2001 by Carus Publishing Company.

Groundwood Books/Douglas & McIntyre Ltd.: "The Great Big Enormous Rock" from *Ten Small Tales* by Celia Barker Lottridge. Text copyright © 1993 by Celia Lottridge.

HarperCollins Publishers: *Ant Cities* by Arthur Dorros. Copyright © 1987 by Arthur Dorros. *Alamo Across Texas* by Jill Stover. Copyright © 1993 by Jill Griffin Stover.

Holiday House, Inc.: *The Ant and the Grasshopper* by Amy Lowry Poole. Copyright © 2000 by Amy Lowry Poole.

National Geographic Society: From *Tricks Animals Play* by Jan Nagel Clarkson. Text copyright © 1975 by National Geographic Society. From *National Geographic Beginner's World Atlas.* Copyright © 1999 by National Geographic Society.

Simon & Schuster Books for Young Readers, Simon & Schuster Children's Publishing Division: *Max* by Rachel Isadora. Copyright © 1976 by Rachel Isadora. *The Little Painter of Sabana Grande* by Patricia Maloney Markun, illustrated by Robert Casilla. Text copyright © 1993 by Patricia Maloney Markun; illustrations copyright © 1993 by Robert Casilla.

Wordsong: "Families, Families" by Dorothy S. Strickland and Michael R. Strickland. Text copyright © 1994 Dorothy S. Strickland and Michael R. Strickland.